Alfred C. Fryer

Llantwit Major

A fifth century University

Alfred C. Fryer

Llantwit Major
A fifth century University

ISBN/EAN: 9783337034658

Printed in Europe, USA, Canada, Australia, Japan

Cover: Foto ©ninafisch / pixelio.de

More available books at **www.hansebooks.com**

LLANTWIT MAJOR

LLANTWIT MAJOR.

LLANTWIT MAJOR:

A Fifth Century University.

BY

ALFRED C. FRYER, Ph.D., M.A.,

Member of Council of the British Archæological Association for Gloucestershire,
Fellow of the Royal Historical Society,

AUTHOR OF
'CUTHBERT OF LINDISFARNE;' 'AIDAN, THE APOSTLE OF THE NORTH.'

LONDON:
ELLIOT STOCK, 62, PATERNOSTER ROW, E.C.
1893.

PREFACE.

DURING the congress of the British Archæological Association, held at Cardiff in 1892, I had the honour to read a paper on 'Llantwit Major: a Fifth Century University;' and in January, 1893, my paper was re-read before the Cardiff Naturalists' Society. This paper has now been enlarged into the present volume, and it is an attempt to give some idea of a university as it existed in the fifth century.

This simple essay claims to be nothing more than a rough sketch; and a series of notes made during a short holiday leisure are here woven together into a few short chapters.

The 'Liber Landavensis,' the Iolo MSS., 'The Lives of the Cambro-British Saints,' and the works of the Rev. W. J. Rees have been freely consulted. I must also express my obligation to Professor Rhys for the use I have made of his work on 'Celtic Heathendom,' and to the Rev. E.

J. Newell for the extracts I have taken from his popular history of the 'Ancient British Church.'

I can scarcely hope to have escaped errors; still, I have done my best to avoid them; those only who are familiar with ancient documents and the difficulties that surround the study of them, can fully appreciate my position in this undertaking.

The knowledge we possess of some of the subjects of study introduced into Chapter IX. is of a later date. This may be considered an anachronism. However, this little book is nothing more than a very rough picture, and the sketch would have been incomplete if some of the studies were not inferred from the knowledge of a somewhat later period, in order to show the kind of teaching that may have been going on at Llantwit in the fifth century.

The subsequent pages contain a sketch of Llantwit and its founders, the students who studied there, and the instruction they may have received.

ALFRED C. FRYER.

CLIFTON, BRISTOL.

CONTENTS.

	PAGE
CHAPTER I.	
LLANTWIT MAJOR	1
CHAPTER II.	
CAER WORGORN	11
CHAPTER III.	
ILLTYD—KNIGHT, HERMIT, AND TEACHER	19
CHAPTER IV.	
STUDENTS: ST. SAMSON OF DOL	31
CHAPTER V.	
STUDENTS: ARMORICAN MISSIONARIES	43
CHAPTER VI.	
STUDENTS AND TEACHERS	55
CHAPTER VII.	
HEATHENDOM	69

CHAPTER VIII.
A UNIVERSITY TOWN - - - - - 83

CHAPTER IX.
STUDY - - - - - 97

CHAPTER X
CONCLUSION - - - - - 121

CHAPTER I
LLANTWIT MAJOR

CHAPTER I.

LLANTWIT MAJOR.

MANY roads across open commons or elevated slopes converge towards the old-world town of Llantwit Major, built in a sheltered hollow near the wild Glamorganshire coast. Before entering the scattered village the traveller catches a glimpse of a fine ruined mansion, and after descending the hill, through narrow streets, between whitewashed cottages and fragments of old houses, he finds himself in a little square, with a gabled inn, some five hundred years old, on his right, while a plain building with a belfry faces him. This ancient building is now used as a town hall, and the bell* bears the inscription '*Sancte Iltute, ora pro nobis.*' Not far from this building is the elongated pile of

---

* Local authorities believe that the bell now in the belfry is the original bell of the saint, with which are connected many legends. However, the size, form, and inscription at once convince us that this bell was cast at a later period when the name of Illtyd had become reverenced. (See *Arch. Cam.*, 1848, p 236.)

the great church. Professor Freeman, in an able paper written for the *Archæologia Cambrensis*,* says: 'The whole series of buildings at Llantwit Major is one of the most striking in the kingdom. Through a succession of civil and domestic structures of the sixteenth and seventeenth centuries, the traveller gradually approaches the grand group composed of the church and the buildings attached to it. Lying as they do in a deep valley below the town, they present a miniature representation of the unequalled assemblage at St. David's.'

The architecture of the present church is not earlier than the thirteenth century, but there is no doubt that it is built on the site of Illtyd's fifth century church. It is indeed a most remarkable accumulation of distinct buildings. The eastern portion is now used as the parish church, and contains traces of frescoes on the wall, an ancient font, and a finely-carved niche. The unique arrangement of the western portions is still a very curious problem. Here are preserved broken and shattered monuments of many an age. Yonder, a finely-carved fragment of a cross has a Latin inscription,† which reads in English: 'In the name

---

* For a full description of the unique arrangement of this thirteenth century church, see Professor Freeman's paper in *Arch. Cam.* for 1858.

† The inscription has given much trouble, but the general intention is plain enough, viz., to commemorate that Howell, in the name of the Trinity, erected the cross for the soul of his father Rhys.

of God the Father and the Son and the Holy Spirit, Howell raised this cross for the soul of his father Rhys.' Howell was a king of Glamorgan, and died in the year 885. In the churchyard are three ancient relics. A curious cylindrical pillar, around which wild, fantastic legends are entwined,* stands against the north wall of the old western church. It is nine feet long, and is carved out of a single piece of sandstone. A straight vertical groove runs the whole way down the back of the stone, and Mr. J. Romilly Allen† feels certain that it formed part of the original design. The pillar is covered with sculpture, and its character shows that it was produced by the same school of early Welsh ecclesiastical artists who designed the other crosses at Llantwit. The top is broken, and it has been suggested that it may have been surmounted by a cross. The groove down the back leaves scope for much speculation. Some have asserted that the pillar was Druidical, and the groove was used to carry away the blood from human victims poured on the top. These stories, however, may be dismissed, as the pillar is a monument of Christian times, and probably dates from the ninth century.

The other ancient relics in the churchyard are

---

* See Donovan's 'Descriptive Excursions through South Wales and Monmouthshire in 1804,' vol. i., p. 340.

† See *Archæologia Cambrensis* for 1889, p. 317.

two inscribed stones. One was raised by Abbot Samson,* 'for his soul and the souls of King Juthael and Arthmael, the dean'; the other is inscribed on one side with the words, 'Samson placed this cross for his soul,' and on the opposite side seems to have the names of Illtyd, Samson, and Samuel, its engraver. These are the remains of finely-carved, ninth century crosses, and Samson and Juthael were well-known people from 846 to 870.

On a hill to the west of the church stands a bald fragment of what was once the gate-house of the mediæval monastery. The curious thirteenth century pigeon-house with its domical vault is still standing; but the ancient tithe-barn has disappeared. In 1858, the solitary gables of this great barn were a conspicuous object, and a writer† of that date remarks: 'On the flat ground of the hill, immediately south of the gate-house, stands the ancient monastic or tithe barn, a vast pile of the thirteenth century. Not many years

---

* See Iolo MSS., p. 363, for an account of how this monument fell into the grave of a young man, who for his great height (7 feet 7 inches), was called 'Will, the Giant.' It appears to have remained in that position for a number of years. The tradition of the stone being underground was not forgotten, and in 1789 it was dug out, and re-erected in 1793 against the east side of the porch. The dimensions of this stone are, 9 feet high, 28 inches wide at bottom, 19 inches wide at top, and 14½ inches thick.

† See *Archæologia Cambrensis*, 1858, p. 186.

ago it was covered with its fine oak roof, in excellent general condition; but at the time of the tithe commutation, the Dean and Chapter of Gloucester, to whom the great tithes belong, were so ill-advised as to allow this roof to be taken down and sold—a glaring, but by no means uncommon, instance of capitular bad taste and ignorant parsimony. As a proof of the value of the tithes, it may be stated that men now living in Llantwit remember seeing this great barn, 122 feet long by 27 feet broad, and as much more to the ridge, filled with corn closely packed, while eleven large wheat stacks encumbered the adjoining field. Now not an ear of corn is ever to be found within the walls. It is all good solid work of the thirteenth century, perfectly plain, but well suited to its purpose. At the present day the walls have been much injured by the villagers, who have pillaged them for stones wherewith to build their houses and fences, the capitular body mentioned above caring nothing for the dilapidation of their property.' The same writer* also mentions that closely connected with the church of Llantwit Major are several buildings belonging to the ecclesiastical establishment of the place. 'On the south side of the churchyard,' he adds, 'and abutting on its present wall, is a house of two stories, standing north and south, which contains

* See *Archæologia Cambrensis*, 1858, p. 184.

niches and doorways of the fourteenth century. It was not very long ago used as a mill, for a small stream, now covered over, runs under it; but it has the appearance rather of a dwelling, and, from its immediate proximity, may have been occupied by some ecclesiastical personages attached to the church. This building has a chimney at the south end, which indicates habitation; whereas the chamber over the south porch of the church does not possess this indispensable article of comfort, though, no doubt, that room, too, was occupied by one of the clerics.' The same writer also tells us that in 1858 there were traces of buildings called collegiate, and a small portion of what is said to have been a cloister in a garden adjoining the whole extent of the northern wall of the churchyard. It was from some spot in this direction that one if not both the ancient incised stones, now erected on the northern side of the church, were carried to their present position.

In a field on the rise of the hill towards the west and north-west of the churchyard, numerous remains of buildings have been found. Local tradition affirms that the college of Llantwit Major formerly stood here, and there is strong probability that this was the site of those famous schools.

This inconsiderable village, so far removed from the workaday world of the nineteenth century,

LLANTWIT MAJOR.

was once of 'great population and eminence.' All around we find remains of an earlier antiquity; fragments of old houses, numerous intersecting streets, grassy mounds covering the foundations of ancient buildings, crosses, memorial and sepulchral, all silently speak of its past greatness. Llantwit may be little known, but its witness is written for all who visit it. Surely the spirits of dead worthies haunt this mysterious place, and surely its story is worth unravelling.

The old buildings of Illtyd's time long ago gave place to others which in their turn have vanished, while the green sward with its daisies and its buttercups cover their foundations. However, the natural features of the landscape are little changed. The brook still meanders to the sea through grassy meadows, the steep slopes of Castle Ditches* are every spring-time glowing masses of golden gorse, while in autumn the red and yellow of the bracken, and the olive-green of countless blades of grass is a miracle of colour. We hear the dull boom, boom, boom, of the angry waves as they break on those foam-fringed cliffs which guard the coast to east and west of Castle Ditches, just as they were heard by those men who lived, laboured, and taught here centuries ago. We see the white gulls circle round the cliffs as if they were never weary of being on the

* This height is crowned by an ancient camp.

wing; we see the blue dome above us with the great clouds sailing majestically across; we see the ever restless, ever changing ocean, now blue, now purple, now a mass of molten gold at sunset. All these things we see to-day, and they gladden our hearts just as they gladdened the heart of Illtyd when he rested from his journey, and 'the delight-some place pleased him well.' The writer of his legend describes the scene. 'Around was no unevenness of mountains or hills, but a most fertile plain of meadows; a wood very thick with different kinds of trees grew therein, and was the resort of many wild animals; a most pleasant river flowed between banks on either hand, and springs intermingled with a rivulet in pleasant courses.' The name of the place was Hodnant, 'the fruitful valley';* it was 'the most beautiful of places.' He who wrote this may have been a Llantwit monk, certainly he was a lover of nature, 'though his admiration,' says a modern writer, 'was rather for the sameness of a level plain and lush meadows where cattle pasture, than for the wild and rugged sublimity of mountain scenery.'†

* The monk's interpretation of the Welsh name has been questioned.
† Newell's 'Ancient British Church' (S. P. C. K.), p. 118.

CHAPTER II
CAER WORGORN

CHAPTER II.

CAER WORGORN.

THE question has often been asked, when was the Christian Faith first preached in Britain? The answer, however, is no easy one, and although many volumes have been written on this subject, the speculations they contain are useless, for early facts are hopelessly interwoven with later fictions. St. Paul's visit to our island is supported on a single sentence of St. Clement of Rome, in which this great apostle is said to 'have come to the boundary of the west.'* The theories respecting British Christian ladies at Rome prove nothing as to a Church in Britain, even if they did not rest on a precarious identification.† The Welsh story, how the Faith of

---

* S. Clem., Ep. ad Cor. 5. The phrase most probably referred to Spain.

† Some have endeavoured to identify Pudens and Claudia of St. Paul's last Epistle with the Pudens and the British-born Claudia, whose marriage Martial greeted in verses published some twenty years after St. Paul's death. (See Martial, Epigr. iv., 13, 1.)

Christ was first brought to the nation of the Cymry from Rome by Bran the Blessed, the father of Caradawc or Caractacus,* is weakened by the lateness of its probable date; and the famous story given by Bede, of how the British King Lucius sent to Eleutherus, Bishop of Rome, a letter, entreating 'that by his commission he might be made a Christian,' seems to be traceable to Rome in the fifth century, and 'this request,' says Professor Bright, 'if made, was made in the latter part of the second century—the accession of Eleutherus being commonly dated A.D. 177.'† The story of how St. Joseph of Arimathea with his twelve companions came to Glastonbury, and how he made his staff take root in the ground and grow into the famous Holy Thorn, can only be received as a beautiful mediæval romance first heard of in Norman times. Tertullian is the first to speak of Christians in Britain. In A.D. 208, he mentions 'parts of Britain not reached by the Romans' as being 'subjected to Christ;' ‡ and Origen, some thirty-one years later, says, 'the light that was to lighten the Gentiles' had now reached even to 'the isles of the sea.'

Welsh chronicles, which are, doubtless, com-

---

* Triad 35, Third Series; see also Triad 62, Third Series.
† 'Early English Church History,' p. 4.
‡ Tertull., adv. Jud. 7.

pilations of earlier traditions, tell us that long before the days of Illtyd a colony of Christians was settled at Caer Worgorn. In 'Achan y Saint' we find the following: 'It was the glory of the Emperor Theodosius, in conjunction with Cystennyn Llydau,* surnamed the Blessed, to have first founded the College of Illtyd, which was regulated by Balerus, a man from Rome; and Padrig, the son of Mawon, was the first principal of it before he was carried away captive by the Irishmen.' This emperor must have been Theodosius II., for neither Theodosius the Elder nor Theodosius the Great were contemporary with Cystennyn Llydaw. It is unfortunate that we cannot accept the tradition that St. Patrick was connected with Côr Tewdws, for his 'Confession' states that he was only sixteen years old when he was made a captive, and so he was too young to be principal of a college.†

In the 'Genealogy of Iestyn ab Gwrgan'‡ we read that Eurgain, daughter of Caradog (Caractacus), founded a school for twelve saints 'near the place now called Llantwit.' St. Ilid at first ordered its policy, and its members went out into different parts of the country to extend the in-

* Constantine.
† See 'Rees' 'Welsh Saints.'
‡ Iolo MSS., p. 343. There is some confusion owing to the intrusion of Caradog quite out of his period, and the recurrence of the name in due order several reigns onward.

fluence of the Church. In the 'Genealogy of the Saints' Ilid is mentioned as a 'man of Isreal,' and is said to have accompanied Bran on his return to his native land. Little is known of Ilid. The church of Llanilid is dedicated to him, and he is said to have retired to the Isle of Avallon, where he died and was buried.

In the reign of Cyllin it is stated that 'many Cambrians became converts to Christianity, through the ministry of the saints of Eurgain's congregation,' and Owain, the son of Cyllin, endowed Côr Eurgain 'with adequate means of subsistence.' In a manuscript compiled in the year 1485 we find it mentioned that 'the College of Theodosius, in Caer Worgorn, was not a monastery, but rather an enfranchised school, to exhibit and teach the distinguished knowledge and exalted sciences that were known in Rome and to the Romans at Caerleon-upon-Usk.'* In this same chronicle we read that the college was rebuilt in the reign of Tewdric, as it had been entirely destroyed by the Saxons, 'so that it became the principal college of all Britain, and the first in the world for learning and piety.' St. German,† saint, soldier, orator, and theologian,

* Iolo MSS., p. 422.

† St. German is said to have come to Britain on his first mission in 429; and on his second in 447; at which period he is considered by some to have instituted the colleges of Llantwit and Llancarfan.

is said to have been the founder of these new schools and to have appointed Illtyd principal. On this point, however, the Welsh records appear to be incorrect, for genealogies prove that Illtyd was too young, and he may rather be said to have lived some eighty years afterwards.* In the ' Liber Landavensis ' we find Illtyd received his appointment from St. Dyfrig, or Dubricius, who lived in an age succeeding that of the famous Bishop of Auxerre.†

St. German played a great part in the history of the British Church, and his remarkable character and undoubted ability have left an indelible impression on the age in which he lived. Various legends and authorities‡ have attributed to him the introduction of the first germs of what afterwards developed into the parochial system,§ and they have also attributed to him the foundations of not only Llantwit and Llancarfan, but also Oxford and Cambridge, as well as the consecration of St. Dyfrig as first bishop of Llandaff and the introduction of the Gallican liturgy into Britain. There is no doubt that this great Gallican bishop marks an era in the history of the British Church. His success in the Pelagian controversy at St.

* *Archæologia Cambrensis*, 1859, p. 57.
† See Rees' 'Welsh Saints,' p. 123.
‡ See Newell's 'Ancient British Church,' p. 24 (S. P. C. K.).
§ See Rees' 'Welsh Saints,' p. 131 ; and Pryce's 'Ancient British Church,' p. 124.

Albans and the part he played in the grand story of the Alleluia Victory have so overshadowed his immediate successors that their individual work and labours have, at a later age, been attributed to this great reformer and administrator. This, no doubt, is the reason that the foundation of Llantwit has been attributed to him and not to St. Dyfrig.

We have seen that these ancient records are in places inconsistent, yet there is little doubt that, either at Llantwit or in its immediate neighbourhood, a seminary was founded at an early date. This continued to exist until the year 446, when the Irish burnt it to the ground. It was rebuilt in the days of St. Dyfrig, and Illtyd was appointed its principal. Under the rule of this remarkable man, who was generally known by the designation of 'excellent master of the Britons,' the place became celebrated. Youths of various nations crowded to his classes, among whom were the sons of British nobles, foreign princes, besides numerous others, amounting at one time to more than two thousand students,* and one tradition even roughly computes the number at three thousand.†

* Iolo MSS., p. 548. † *Ibid.*, p. 556.

CHAPTER III

ILLTYD KNIGHT, HERMIT, AND TEACHER

CHAPTER III.

ILLTYD—KNIGHT, HERMIT, AND TEACHER.

OF all those truly great men who lived during the troubled period of the fifth and sixth centuries there are few whose story is so quaint and so strange as that of Illtyd, knight, hermit, scholar, and principal of a great school of learning. The legends told by his primitive biographers* are so fantastic and so tragical that it is no easy matter to separate the chaff from the wheat. Still, through all the absurdity of later romances we are able to see that Illtyd possessed the elements of true sincerity, virtue, and nobility.

He appears to have been born in Armorica, and

* The oldest accounts of Illtyd are to be found in the lives of SS. Gildas, Samson, and Maglorius, written about the year 600, and published in Mabillon's 'Acta Sanctorum Ordinis S. Benedicti,' Venice, 1733, i. 131, 154 seq., 209. See also 'Life of St. Samson' in 'Liber Landavensis.' A life of St. Illtyd is to be found in Cottonian MSS., Vespasian, A. xiv. This MS. was written in the eleventh or twelfth century. It is printed in Rees' 'Cambro-British Saints,' and abridged in Capgrave's 'Nova Legenda Angliæ,' fol. clxxxvii.

was the son of Bicanys by a sister* of Emyr Llydaw; he was, therefore, the great-nephew of St. German the famous Bishop of Auxerre.

The old chronicler tells us that Bicanys† was a celebrated soldier, that he was beloved by king d queen, and that he possessed considerable influence in the palace.

His boy would seem to have been well educated, like others of his class, and we are told he was 'instructed in the seven sciences.' His memory, even at this early age, appears to have been remarkable, and his eloquence has also been commented on by his biographer.

He followed his father in the profession of arms, crossed from Armorica to King Arthur's court, and afterwards came to Glamorgan, attaching himself for a time to the court of the regulus of that district. He must have distinguished himself in his profession, for he became known as Illtyd Farchog, or Illtyd the knight. The chronicler adds: 'Outwardly he was a soldier who wore a military dress, but inwardly he was one of the most intelligent of the natives of Britain. Therefore he was appointed by King Paulinus to be chief over the soldiers, on account of his exquisite

---

* John of Teignmouth calls her Riengulida; in another account she is called Gweryla, daughter of Tewdrig, king of Glamorgan.

† 'Ex quibus claruit Bicanus, miles famosissimus, illustris genere, et in armis militaribus.'

eloquence and incomparable intelligence: no contemporary could be compared with him for mental ability, which was proved and confirmed by the testimony of learned men.'

One day he joined the king's family in a hunt, in the course of which they came upon the territory of St. Cadoc of Llancarfan. Illtyd's comrades extorted bread, beer, and a fat pig from Cadoc the Wise; and their insolence, the legend says, was punished, for the earth opened and swallowed them up. It may have been that Illtyd's friends were standing on badly drained and marshy land, and, like the wicked Cefygid,* they disappeared in a rushy swamp. Perhaps it was a glow of feeling which followed this solemn event, or perhaps it was the wish to overcome his weakness and his failings that moved Illtyd the knight to that last extremity of self-devotion known to the age in which he lived. At any rate, Cadoc, his kinsman, easily persuaded him to renounce the world and embrace the hermit life.

As the call had come to St. Antony two hundred years before, when he heard the Gospel words: 'If thou wilt be perfect, go and sell that thou hast, and give to the poor, and thou shalt have treasure in heaven, and come and follow Me,' so, too, it came to Illtyd, bidding him lead a life of poverty and self-restraint, ever practising good deeds

'Vita Sancti Iltuti,' xx.

towards his fellow-men. No wonder men in the fifth century fled from the world and tried to be alone with God. Europe was a chaos; Rome had been sacked; the Teutonic tribes were growing stronger and stronger; bands of robbers infested the land; the amusements of the people were either tasteless or brutal; and all around were tawdry luxury, cunning intrigue, and bloody warfare.

The hermits were the heroes of their age. Strong as giants, with axe and spade in hand, they overcame the natural difficulties of bog and forest, and withal they possessed a personal love for Christ, and a faith in the Unseen, which has never been equalled. Charles Kingsley tells us that 'their influence, subtle, often transformed and modified again and again, but still potent from its very subtleness, is being felt around us in many a puzzle—educational, social, political; and promises to be felt still more during the coming generation.'

Very literally did these men follow the words of our Lord; and the text, 'He that loveth father and mother more than Me is not worthy of Me; and he that loveth son or daughter more than Me is not worthy of Me,' came upon Illtyd with such force that it led to a sad and pathetic incident. In terror he fled into the forest from Trynihid, his fair young wife. He would not even allow her to share his hut made of branches, and for some

ST. ILLTYD'S CROSS (LLANTWIT MAJOR).

time she could not find him. At last she discovered him making an immense dyke of mud and stones to keep out the inundations of a neighbouring river. The poor wife at first scarcely knew her once gay knight, for he was now poorly dressed and covered with mud. So she went away and never saw him more, 'fearing,' as the chronicler said 'to displease God and one so beloved of God.'*

The Legendary Life narrates a pretty story of how King Merichion was hunting a stag, when the poor frightened creature fled into Illtyd's cell. The protection it sought was willingly given, and the hermit refused to give it up to the angry king. Afterwards the stag remained with its protector, sharing his solitude, and assisting him to carry wood from the forest by drawing a cart laden with timber.†

From the charm of legendary stories we turn to some facts in the life of Illtyd which appear to be historical. We may take it for granted that he had been a distinguished soldier, having earned the proud title of 'knight,' and that he had

* She retired to the mountains, and lived a religious life there. 'She built a habitation, and formed an oratory . . . and continued to live devoutly, comforting innumerable widows and poor nuns.'

† Compare the legends of St. Marculph and the hare, St. Gilles and the doe, St. Malo and the wren, St. Calais and the buffalo, St. Deicolus and the boar.

suddenly abandoned his profession, being persuaded by Cadoc the Wise to embrace the hard struggling existence of a Celtic hermit. We may also consider as historical facts that Illtyd was ordained by St. Dyfrig, or Dubricius, Bishop of Llandaff; that he built a church,* became the head of a Celtic monastery,† and was also the principal of a great school of learning which was in every sense of the word a university long before Oxford or Cambridge became famous.

The name of Illtyd is also honoured by the Welsh on account of his having introduced among them an improved method of ploughing; before his era they were accustomed to cultivate their ground with the mattock and over-treading plough (aradr arsang), implements which, the compiler of the 'Triad' upon husbandry observes, were still used by the Irish.‡

The Legendary Life§ tells us that on a certain night two robbers stole a number of pigs belonging to Illtyd. However, they lost their way, and

---

* See Rees' 'Welsh Saints' for a list of the churches founded by St. Illtyd.

† The monastery was called Caer Worgorn, and Côr Tewdws; sometimes Bangor Illtyd (Illtyd's College), which name led Montalembert ('Monks of the West,' Bk. viii., c. ii.), followed by Kingsley ('Hermits,' p. 249), to confound it with Bangor Iscoed on the Dee.

‡ 'Triad' 56, Third Series.

§ 'Vita Sancti Iltuti,' xxiii.

the pigs, weary and hungry, returned to their home. The next evening, during the hours of darkness, the robbers again stole the pigs, but this time both robbers and pigs were turned into stones. 'This memorable miracle,' says the eleventh century chronicler, 'is believed by posterity; for hitherto the place of the pigsty is seen, and has the name of Illtyd; and there are also to be seen two immovable stones under the name of two robbers, and it is believed that the robbers were changed into these hard stones.' So writes this mediæval biographer; and doubtless the legend owes its origin to some circle of stones once dedicated to Druidic rites.

The early Celtic Christians had the highest veneration for small quadrangular, portable handbells made of iron and bronze.* The bells† so highly reverenced on our island during the

---

* See *Archæologia Cambrensis*, 1848, p. 230.

† Legend says that St. Teilo's bell convicted the perjured, healed the sick, and sounded every hour of itself until the charm was broken by polluted hands. In the 'Liber Landavensis' we read that Oudoceus turned some butter into a golden bell, which was long preserved in the Church of Llandaff. Gildas brought a wonderful bell from Ireland which he intended to give to the Bishop of Rome. On his way he visited St. Cadoc at Llancarfar, who made several vain attempts to obtain the bell. When Gildas at length arrived at Rome, the bishop asked him to take the present back to St. Cadoc. This was done, and the bell long continued to be one of the wonders of Wales on account of its efficiency in discovering theft and exposing falsehood.

Middle Ages, were doubtless relics of these founders of early Christianity. Giraldus Cambrensis, in his Welsh Itinerary, says that 'both the laity and clergy in Ireland, Scotland and Wales, held in such veneration certain portable bells, that they were more afraid of swearing falsely by them than by the Gospels, because of some hidden and miraculous power with which they were gifted; and by the vengeance of the saint to whom they were pleasing, their despisers and transgressors were severely punished.'

St. Illtyd's bell is perhaps the most renowned of all the wonder-working bells belonging to Celtic saints. The biographer of his legendary life tells us that the saint had retired from Llantwit, and was praying and meditating in a certain cave when a messenger from Gildas the historian passed, carrying a brazen bell which he was sending as a present to his friend David, Bishop of Menevia. The bell sounded miraculously when the messenger came near the cave. Illtyd heard it, came and spoke to the man, and sounded the bell three times. When the messenger gave the precious bell into the hands of the bishop it emitted no sound when it was struck. The man mentioned what had happened on the way, and David exclaimed: 'I know that our master Illtyd wished to possess it, on account of the sweetness of its sound, but he would not ask for it, having heard

Illtyd—Knight, Hermit, and Teacher

that it was sent to me as a gift from Gildas.' So the bell was sent back to Illtyd,* and its further history forms many chapters of wonderful legends.

The year in which Illtyd died is uncertain.† Tradition affirms that he was buried near the chapel that bears his name in Brecknockshire, where there is a place called *Bedd Gwyl Illtyd*,‡ or the grave of St. Illtyd's eve, from its having been a custom to watch there during the night previous to the saint's day.§ The Legendary Life, however, tells us that in the eventide of his days he returned to his native land, and commending his spirit to the Lord, he died at Dol 'on the eighth of the Ides of November.'‖

Thus ended the life of Illtyd—a life filled with one great master-thought, the desire to do the will of Christ. For this he gave up everything that made the existence of a fifth century knight sweet and pleasant, and chose the hard, bitter lot

---

* 'Vita Sancti Iltuti,' xix.
† See Rees' 'Welsh Saints.'
‡ Jones' 'Brecknockshire,' vol. ii., p. 683.
§ Some have conjectured he died in A.D. 480; but it is evident that his life extended through a considerable part of the sixth century. According to Cressy his commemoration was held on February 7th, but he is usually commemorated on November 6:h. (See Alban Butler, vol. xi. ; also 'Vita Sancti Iltuti,' xxiv.)
‖ 'Vita Sancti Iltuti,' xxiv

of a Celtic hermit. But the Lord had other work for him to do, and he was called forth to influence the age in which he lived in a very remarkable way. The school of learning which he founded is said, at one time, to have numbered as many as three thousand students;* while scholars and bards, historians and poets, dignified ecclesiastics and zealous missionaries came under his strong magnetic influence. His age is not ours, and we must make some allowance for incidents in his life which may appear fantastical, or even at times unmeaning. It is not often that the memory of a man famous for his educational influence is held in enthusiastic veneration by the peasantry. This, however, has been the case with Illtyd, and nothing has been more common than to name their children after this great man. Those missionaries who have shown the deepest interest in everyday concerns have had the most powerful influence, and Illtyd was an illustration of this.

* Iolo MSS., p. 556.

CHAPTER IV

STUDENTS: ST. SAMSON OF DOL

CHAPTER IV.

STUDENTS: ST. SAMSON OF DOL.

A UNIVERSITY has been defined* as a body of studious and learned men, competent to pronounce a judgment on the subjects which form a part of the academical course of reading and instruction, and (by their collection in one place) concentrating a flood of light on these subjects. Such was Llantwit Major, and as we glance at the lives of some of those men who studied there in the fifth and sixth centuries, we shall see that it was in truth a luminous point, diffusing its rays in all directions over the rest of the community.

One of its most famous students was St. Samson,† Bishop of Dol. This remarkable man

---

* 'Influence of Authority in Matters of Opinion,' by Sir G. C. Lewis, p. 338.

† See 'Ancient Life,' by Bishop Tigernomail, who lived at the same time or shortly after, also Life in ' Liber Landavensis,' i. 8, c. 25 ; and Du Bosc, ' Bibloth. Floriac.,' 464-484. There also appears to have been another Life attributed to Balderic, Bishop of Dol, who died in 1130.

was born in Siluria about the year 525: and he was the son of Amwn, by Anna, daughter of Meurig ap Tewdrig, Prince of Glamorgan.

Amwn and Anna were some time without a child; but, when Amwn presented three silver bars to the Church, Anna dreamt that she should have a son, who would be seven times more precious than the bars of silver given for him.

At the age of five Samson was placed under the care of Illtyd, and while at Llantwit he must have been industrious, for we read that he was taught 'all the Old and New Testaments, and all sorts of philosophy, to wit, geometry and rhetoric, grammar and arithmetic, and all the arts known in Britain.'

One of the first of a series of charming legends is to be found in the 'Liber Landavensis.' The legend states that one day when the boys were out winnowing corn with the steward, an adder darted out of a bramble bush suddenly and struck one of the monks, who fainted with fright.

'Run, one of you boys, and tell Illtyd,' said the steward. Samson ran with tears in his eyes to tell the news, and full of faith and enthusiasm he asked to be allowed to attempt the cure. Illtyd gave him permission, and Samson ran back and rubbed the bite with oil. By degrees the monk got over his fright and the adder's bite, and Samson was thought much of after this.

Like many of the Celtic saints, Samson possessed a great affection for the animal world. Attached to the school was a cornfield,* and during the autumn the boys took it in turn to drive the sparrows away. At length Samson, who was a great favourite of Illtyd's, took his turn to take care of the corn. He collected all the sparrows and took them into the barn, and, having shut the door, he returned to the cornfield and fell asleep. His companions, who were evidently very jealous of him, ran and told Illtyd that the boy he was so fond of was 'lazy and disobedient.' Illtyd accompanied the boys to the cornfield, awoke the sleeper, and asked him if he had killed the sparrows with his sling; but it was soon discovered how he had collected them and placed them in the barn. Many years after, when the schoolboy had become Bishop of Dol, we read that his monks were disturbed by the cries of the wild birds, so one night he collected them together in the court of the monastery, imposing silence upon them, and the next morning he dismissed them.

Several years passed in labour and study; and at last the day for his ordination as deacon arrived, and Dubricius, Bishop of Caerleon, came to Llantwit. When Samson knelt before the altar, a white pigeon which he had doubtless fed and fondled, flew in at the window and settled on

* See 'Liber Landavensis.'

his shoulder. There the bird remained until the young deacon was ordained, and he arose after receiving the Holy Communion.

Illtyd had two nephews at Llantwit. One was a priest, and the other was butler in the monastery. The priest was very jealous and feared that he would not succeed his uncle on his death, if Samson were at Llantwit. So he and his brother determined to kill him. Now it was the custom for the butler to prepare for the monks a cooling drink of crushed herbs,* to purify their blood. The butler placed some poisonous herb in the young deacon's cup, but Samson let the cat† lap some of it, and the animal died. The question has been asked: 'Was the butler a foreigner, and Samson suspicious of a novelty?'

After Samson was ordained priest, he asked Illtyd to allow him to live on a little island near Llantwit, where Piro, 'a holy priest and excellent man,'‡ resided. Illtyd gave him leave, for he knew that his favourite disciple longed to lead a more austere life, and craved for quiet. Samson worked hard all day with his hands, and at night he studied in his little cell by the light of his oil lantern.

* 'Tillium.'
† 'Pilax.'
‡ 'A quodam egregio viro de sancto presbytero, Piro nomine.'

SAMSON'S CROSS (LLANTWIT MAJOR).

While Samson was on the island he received news that his father was ill and desired to see him. At first he refused to go, but Piro reasoned with him, and he set out, accompanied by a young deacon as his companion. They rode through a vast forest, and the hooting of the owls and other strange noises which echoed through the interlacing arches filled them with fears. An old woman with flowing gray hair and a huge boar-spear in her hand so alarmed the young deacon that he beat his horse and galloped along the rough road. His horse stumbled, he was thrown off, and he lay insensible on the ground. Samson crossed himself, caught the old woman, and asked her who she was. She replied that she was a witch, and Samson told her that she had not long to live, whereat, the chronicle adds, 'she gave a precipitous leap, fell down, and expired.' The young man was restored to consciousness, they proceeded on their journey, and Samson remarked, 'You were lucky not to be transfixed with her great spear, my friend.'

On reaching his father's house, Amwn ordered everyone out of the room, except his wife, his son, and the deacon, and he then made a confession of the sins of his past life. He vowed to dedicate himself, his wife, Samson's six brothers, and his baby daughter to the Lord; and on his recovery to health Samson placed them in cells, where they might learn monastic discipline.

Samson returned to Llantwit, and the young deacon told Illtyd all that had befallen them on the way, 'not concealing his own cowardice.' Illtyd was so well pleased with his favourite disciple that he appointed him cellarer. This created discontent, and it was soon hinted that Samson had a sweet tooth and ate the honey out of the jars. So Illtyd went to the store-room, examined the jars, and found they were full.

About this time a sad event took place. Piro, that 'excellent man and holy priest,' one night imbibed too much strong drink, and returning to his cell stumbled and fell into the well. His howling soon attracted attention; he was hauled out, but he died from the bruises and broken bones he had received. After this Samson was elected to succeed Piro as head of the island monastery, and he endeavoured by his own example to instil into the brothers a love of temperance both in food and drink.* His monks opposed his reforms, and after a year and a half he visited Ireland, and on his return he led the life of a hermit in a lone cave on the shore of the 'Severn sea.' One night he dreamt that he saw three bishops in glittering vestments and golden

* 'Studebat inter dapes abundantes et pocula inundantia jejunus semper ac sitiens esse.'

mitres on their heads. They were the Apostles St. Peter, St. James and St. John, and they recited the office of consecrating bishops over him. He at once went to St. Dubricius and informed him of the vision; and the Bishop of Caerleon consecrated him and two others to the office of bishops in his cathedral.*

Soon after his consecration he sailed to Armorica. He took ship to Brittany, and on landing he filled his cart with his books and vestments, and harnessed to it 'two horses which he had brought from Ireland.' One day he passed a crowd of Bretons making merry and dancing round an upright granite stone. Samson sprang from his cart and denounced this relic of paganism. The revellers laughed at him; but a boy who was galloping about on the back of a horse was thrown off. He was taken up insensible, and the scoffers' mockery was exchanged into lamentations. Samson knelt down by the child, and soon after he returned to consciousness. The saint carved a cross on the granite stone, and his biographer informs us that he had both seen and felt it.

Samson's wanderings came to an end; he

---

* One chronicle states that St. Dubricius declared it unnecessary to re-ordain one who had received episcopal orders from the hands of the Apostles. However, the 'Liber Landavensis' states that he was ordained by St. Dubricius.

settled at Dol, and erected a monastery. Here he replaced a forest with fruit trees, and with the help of Telio, a British monk, he planted an orchard three miles in extent.* Here he kept bees to such good purpose, that one day he told the Bishop of Paris that they not only had at Dol an abundant supply of honey, but they had actually more wax than they could use in the church during the whole year. However, he could not grow vines, so the bishop arranged to take his surplus wax to light his church in Paris, in exchange for wine grown on his more southern estates.

Jonas, prince of that part of Brittany, had been killed, and the usurper, Commor, had sent the son of Jonas, named Judael, to King Childebert, at Paris. Samson went specially to Paris to beg the king to release the young prince and reinstate him in his possessions. However, he met with strong opposition from Queen Ultrogotha,† who endeavoured to poison him.‡ Never-

---

* This orchard existed in the twelfth century under the name of *Arboretum Teliavi et Samsonis*. To them is attributed the introduction of apple trees into Armorica, where cider continues to be the national drink.

† Rev. S. Baring-Gould, in his 'Lives of the Saints,' says: 'All this latter part of the narrative appears to have been tampered with by copyists, who have inserted stories of his conquering lions and dragons.'

‡ See 'Liber Landavensis.'

theless he carried his point, and Judael was restored to his principality.

The story which represented St. Samson having been Archbishop of York and then at Menevia is, says Professor Bright, a myth of a later date; the fact being simply that he was consecrated in Wales, and thence proceeded to Armorica, and sat in a council of Paris in 557.*

The life of St. Samson by Tigernomail† leaves us to infer that he died at Dol,‡ and the 'Liber Landavensis' states that he was attacked by severe illness at that place, and passed away surrounded by his sorrowing disciples. The Welsh accounts, however, say that he returned from Armorica to the college at Llantwit, where he died.

A glance at Armorica in the period under review will show us what Samson and his followers had to encounter. The population had diminished, and the people had almost discontinued to till the

* See 'Chapters of Early Church History,' p. 32; see also Haddan and Stubbs, i., 149, 159.

† This ancient 'Life' is attributed to a Bishop Tigernomail, of St. Paul de Léon. It is fairly trustworthy and very curious, and agrees in many particulars with the one in the 'Liber Landavensis,' i., 8, c. 25. The author had been a student at Llantwit. He says, 'in cujus magnifico monasterio ego fui.' The later lives are based on this one, with increased number of marvels.

‡ Alban Butler says he died in 564, but this is evidently inaccurate. He died, according to some authorities, in 593, at the age of 68.

soil. The villages had ceased to exist, and the very site of many of the towns could only be traced under a mass of tangled underwood. The baths and villas, temples and streets, were crumbling ruins, and chaos ruled everywhere. It was at this critical period that Samson and other Llantwit students came to Armorica. Samson settled at Dol, proclaimed the Divine message to the people who dwelt around, helped them in their agricultural labours, and taught them the first principles of civilization. He and his followers made with their own hands civilized dwellings; and at a time when blood-feuds were everyday things, when chieftains rose and fell, and all seemed change, chaos, and storm, schools were established, the Scriptures studied, and the Sacraments of the Christian Church administered. When Samson closed his eyes in death, he left behind him the visible memorials of a noble life, and in those dark times we see how the Lord of the harvest was pleased *to send forth labourers into His harvest.**

* St. Matt. ix. 38.

CHAPTER V

STUDENTS: ARMORICAN MISSIONARIES

CHAPTER V.

STUDENTS : ARMORICAN MISSIONARIES.

BESIDES St. Samson of Dol, the names of many Llantwit students are still held in loving memory by the good folk of Brittany. St. Leonore, St. Paul of Léon, St. Maglorius, and many others received an education at Llantwit which fitted them for the arduous labours of a missionary life. Labour and prayer was their rule at Llantwit, and labour and prayer was their rule in Armorica.

With spade in hand they wandered forth into those vast solitudes, and near some bubbling stream they cleared a patch of land sufficient to be sown or to become a meadow. Their clearings extended, and groves of oaks were replaced by cornfields. Such labour required all their energy, and their perseverance was rewarded, for they were never known to abandon any land they had once undertaken to reclaim. We are told[*] that

[*] See Montalembert's 'Monks of the West,' vol. ii., p. 371.

they carried labour and fertility, human strength and intelligence into those dreary wastes or darksome forests, transforming the woods and thickets into pastures and cornfields. This was, indeed, a dramatic struggle with the forces of nature; and we see these brave men overcoming every obstacle and danger—living in marshes, opening up roads through the great masses of forest, and bringing land into regular cultivation.

Sometimes they replaced a forest with fruit trees,* or a thicket with vines. They were their own carpenters and masons, as well as gardeners. Many a one ground his own wheat, and many a one formed a fishpond round the well he had discovered. 'If any man would not work neither should he eat,' said the great Apostle; and the Psalmist's words, 'Thou shalt eat the labour of thy hands,' was the keynote of their daily existence. *Cruce et aratro* might in very truth have been emblazoned on the banner of these Christian civilizers.

One of this noble band was Leonore. At an early age he was placed under the care of Illtyd, and he is said to have become one of his most distinguished students. The ancient records tell us that he became an accomplished calligraphist, and that he possessed brilliant abilities. He

* St. Samson and Telio planted an orchard at Dol, three miles in extent.

appears to have been consecrated a bishop while he was young, for in a later age he is known as 'the boy bishop.' The call came to him to evangelize the Celts of Armorica, and he left Llantwit accompanied by seventy-three disciples.

Crossing over into Brittany, they entered into a close conflict with nature; and these brave men, without arms, and with few implements, plunged into those terrible forests. This, indeed, required a courage of which we have no idea, for the stories of dreaded phantoms were very real to those men; the howling of wolves often accompanied their praises to God, while bands of armed robbers were constantly to be met with. But the faith of Leonore and his disciples was strong in the living God, and the work He had given them to do. Thus they wandered through sombre and impenetrable forests, through copses of aspen and birch, through cruel thickets of bramble and thorn. At last, when they rested in some hollow or on some barren fell, Leonore may have prayed like Sequanus: 'Lord, who hast made heaven and earth, who hearest the prayers of him who comes to Thee, from whom everything good proceeds, and without whom all the efforts of human weakness are vain; if Thou ordainest me to establish myself in this solitude, make it known to me, and lead to a good issue the beginning which Thou hast already granted to my devotion.'

'The legend of St. Leonore,' says Montalembert, 'is one of the finest pearls from the casket of Celtic tradition.' The young bishop and his disciples founded a rude monastery in a valley of moorland, and having thatched their wattled cells with red fern, they built a rustic chapel. With lichen-covered stones they constructed a byre for their cattle; they stacked the turf for use in winter days; they drained the swampy marsh, praying ever as they laboured; and then they ploughed the land, but, alas! they had no grain.

> 'Said the Bishop: "God will help us
>   In the hour of bitter loss."
> Then one spied a Robin Redbreast
>   Sitting on a wayside cross.
>
> 'Doubtless came the bird in answer!
>   To the words the monk did speak,
> For a heavy wheat-ear dangled
>   From the Robin's polished beak.
>
> 'Then the brothers, as he dropped it,
>   Picked it up and careful sowed;
> And abundantly in autumn,
>   Reaped the harvest where they strewed.'*

Such is the popular tradition among the simple folk of Brittany. Another version, however, says that a little white bird, which carried in its beak an ear of corn, settled at the feet of Leonore. He

---

* 'The Silver Store,' by the Rev. S. Baring-Gould.

thanked God, and bid one of his disciples follow the bird, and in a glade in the neighbouring forest he found a store of grain.

The author* of 'The Silver Store' ends his charming poem with the following lines:

> 'Do you mark the waving glory
>   O'er the Breton hill-slopes flung?
> All that wealth from Robin Redbreast's
>   Little ear of wheat has sprung.
>
> 'Do you mark the many churches
>   Scattered o'er that pleasant land?
> All results are of the preaching
>   Of that venerable band.
>
> 'Therefore, Christian, small beginnings
>   Pass not by with lip of scorn;
> God may prosper them, as prospered
>   Robin Redbreast's ear of corn.'†

Few of these missionary apostles have received more respect than that Paul‡ who has given his name to the city of St. Paul de Léon. He was the son of a Welsh prince, and was educated at Llantwit. However, at the age of sixteen he crossed the sea into Brittany, where he built an oratory and a cell. In time other young and

* Rev. S. Baring-Gould.

† 'Robin Redbreast's corn' is a by-word in Brittany for small beginnings that prosper.

‡ A 'Life' of St. Paul of Léon was written by Worwonock, monk of Landevenec, in the ninth century. This was re-written in the following century by an anonymous monk of the Abbey of Feury.

ardent spirits joined him. With axe in hand they felled the giant trees around them, cleared away copse and brushwood, dug and weeded the soil, and prepared it for sewing their grain. The wild animals had no fear of these kind and gentle denizens of the forest, and many later stories owe their origin to these sylvan traditions. Thus St. Paul of Léon is said to have tamed a ferocious she-bear, compelled an unruly buffalo to return to the forest, and forced a crocodile or sea-serpent to throw itself into the sea.* We can trace, however, some of his real labours even beneath the fantastic legends of a later age. One strange story tells how he increased the size of an island to please his sister, by ordering the sea to draw back four hundred paces, and how the new boundary was marked with pebbles which his sister laid round the land, and strewed down the road she and her brother had taken. And lo! the pebbles grew into tall pillars of stone, and the avenue is still called the road of St. Paul. It is easy to understand that the missionary bishop superintended some great embankment which the Morbihan peasant clothed with a romantic legend; while the story of the stones growing out of pebbles explains the existence of the druidical circles and avenues.

* On the coast there is a whirlpool still called ' L'Abîme du Serpent.'

TOWN HALL (LLANTWIT MAJOR).

His practical teaching may be seen in other stories. In the island of Batz, Paul settled for a time, and we read that he found wild bees in the hollow of a tree. They were swarming, so he gathered the swarm, set them in a hive, and taught the people how to collect honey. He also tamed a wild sow, and doubtless this legend points to his having taught the peasants to keep pigs.

In art, St. Paul of Léon is represented either with a bell, or with a cruse of water and a loaf of bread, or driving a dragon into the sea.

The good bishop had long wished to possess a bell, and one day when he was with Count Withur, a fisherman brought the Count a bell he had picked up on the shore, and which the Count gave to the bishop. 'That bell,' says his historian, 'has received from the people a special name, on account of its colour and shape, for it is green and oblong.' He is also represented with a cruse of water and a loaf of bread, as he is said to have lived on nothing else; while his driving a dragon into the sea is thought to signify that he expelled the druidical superstition out of Armorica.

Another member of this noble band of missionaries was Maglorius,* in Welsh, Maelor. He

* The 'Life of Maglorius' is full of fable written not later than the tenth century. (See Mabillon, 'Acta,' SS. O.S.B., t. i.)

was a relation of St. Samson of Dol, and was placed at an early age under the care of Illtyd. When his studies at Llantwit were completed, he crossed over to Brittany and was ordained by St. Samson, and on his death he succeeded him as Bishop of Dol.

When Maglorius was very old he conferred his pastoral staff on Budoc, as he longed to end his days in a quiet place, where he could pray and meditate undisturbed by the multitudes who flocked to him. But crowds of men and women, eager for instruction and help, sought out his place of retirement, and life became a burden to the aged man. He poured out his troubles to Budoc, who quickly reminded him that he could not deny the poor of Christ the true seed of spiritual life, nor refuse to take upon himself the burden of the people's sorrows. So, again, we read of him as the head of a large community, ready and willing to labour for the Lord until the Master's call came, and he was free to go to Him.

Like many other Celtic teachers, Maglorius was a man overflowing with sympathy for all God's creatures, wherever and howsoever he encountered them. He was a friend of everything that rejoiced or suffered, and his boundless sympathy attracted birds and animals to him, just as six centuries later the same sympathetic power attracted the little birds and wild creatures of the wood and fields to Francis of Assisi.

> 'He prayeth best who loveth best
> All things both great and small;
> For the dear God who loveth us,
> He made and loveth all.'

This was the unconscious creed of Maglorius, as it was equally the unconscious creed of the great prophet of Assisi. The animals and birds trusted him; they had no fear of him, neither was he afraid of them. The following amusing story is told of him. Count Soiesco, owner of the island of Sargo, now known as Jersey, was afflicted with leprosy; Maglorius healed him, and in gratitude the Count gave him half the island. However, the wild fowl and the fish deserted the Count's portion for that of the Saint. The Count, and more particularly his wife, were dismayed, and begged that Maglorius should change with them. But when the exchange was made the birds and fishes immediately followed Maglorius, going and coming, so as always to keep in his portion. The legend adds that at last the Count abandoned the whole island and gave it to Maglorius.

The people besought these good Celtic missionaries to cure all their ills—whether of body or of soul. 'You ask too much of a sinful man,' exclaimed an anchorite in the great Desert of Perche, when a father brought his crippled child to be cured. So, too, said Maglorius when a count, rich in a hundred ploughs and possessing innumerable fishing boats, asked him to restore his daughter's speech: 'My son,' answered Maglorius, 'trouble me not: that which you ask is beyond the power of our weakness. When I am sick, I know not whether I am to die or be cured. How, then, having no power over my own life, should I be able to take away any of the other calamities permitted by God? Return to your house and offer abundant alms to God, that you may obtain from Him the cure of your daughter.'

* * * * *

These scholars from Llantwit went forth into a land of murder and arson, carnage and misrule; but their self-sacrificing lives became centres of Christian influence, and moral life again revived in a land which for five centuries had been under the dominion of Roman emperors; while everywhere, in thatch-covered churches and under the interlacing branches of druidical groves, the Holy Eucharist was celebrated. These sons of Llantwit, disciples of Illtyd, taught the same arts in Armorica they had learnt in Siluria, and were led by the same faith and hope—the faith once delivered to the saints and the hope that springs out of it.

CHAPTER VI

STUDENTS AND TEACHERS

CHAPTER VI.

STUDENTS AND TEACHERS.

WE now turn to glance over the names of some other famous men who were connected with Llantwit, either as students or as teachers.

Gildas,* the Wise, seems to have studied in these famous schools about the time that St. Paul of Léon was a student, although he was somewhat younger than the Breton missionary. The author of the life of St. Paul of Léon calls Gildas the brightest genius of the school of St. Illtyd. No doubt he was a remarkable man, but he possessed a gloomy temper, which was irritated by the triumphs of the Saxon foemen. He was pre-eminently an ecclesiastic, and fully conscious of the vices of his countrymen. He crossed to Brittany not later than 550, and while he was

---

* Both the Breton and Welsh 'Lives' are untrustworthy, and legendary in character. The one was written by a monk of Ruys, and is of a late date; the other by Caradog of Llancarfan.

there he wrote his celebrated work which Alcuin*
twice refers to in his Epistle, calling its author
'the wisest of the Britons,' while Bede† styles
him 'the historian of the Britons.' There is a
grandeur in the boldness of this Celtic Jeremiah;
and 'the princes he withstood,' says a modern
author, 'were not respectable hypocrites, nor cold
philosophers, or careless worldlings, to whom
religion was contemptible; they bore with meekness the reproofs of God's servants; they could
feel, and feel deeply, conviction of sin. The conversion of Cystennin, which was one of the most
remarkable events of the sixth century,‡ may have
been the result of the admonitions of Gildas's
" Epistle," and was thorough and permanent.'§
These princes were not as the rich who are sent
empty away, the mighty who are put down from
their seats. They were passionate men and
sinners. They listened to the voice of the
Church, and their repentance was true and
sincere. The gifts they gave to the Church were
royal gifts, but they were never considered as
atonement for sin, for the Celtic Church demanded holiness of life from all its members.

Tradition connects the name of Gildas with

* Jaffé, 'Monumenta Alcuiniana' in Bibl. Rer. Germ. vi., 206, 371.
† 'Hist. Eccl.,' lib. i., chap. xxii.
‡ A.D. 589 ('Annales Cambriæ').
§ Newell's 'Ancient British Church,' p. 113.

Brittany, and it seems not unlikely that he was the founder of the monastery of St. Gildas at Ruys.*

The famous St. David,† or Dewi, as the Welsh call him, was educated at Llantwit, before he studied the Scriptures for ten years with Paul Hên at Whitland,‡ in Carmarthenshire. Tradition says that while he had been learning the Scriptures from Paul Hên, he had never ventured to look up at the face of his master. Certainly, he led a very quiet and retired life, and it was not until considerable pressure was exerted that he attended the Synod of Brefé, convened by Dubricius in the year 519. At this synod David made a famous speech, full of grace and eloquence, 'and while he was speaking,' says a beautiful yet wild legend, 'a snow-white dove descending from heaven sat upon his shoulders; and, moreover, the earth on which he stood raised itself under him until it became a hill, from whence his voice was heard like a trumpet, and was understood by all, both near and

---

* Gildas died in 569 or 570.

† There are no very ancient accounts of St. David. The 'Life' in a MS. at Utrecht is the oldest. There are also 'Lives' by Ricimer, Giraldus, and John of Tynemouth. Ricimer was Bishop of St. David's, and died about 1096. Several MSS. of this 'Life' are extant. Giraldus Cambrensis wrote his 'Life of St. David' about 1177. St. Kentigern (died 590) mentions St. David.

‡ Ty Givyn was the foundation of Bishop Paulinus, or Paul Hên.

far off: on the top of which hill a church was afterwards built, and remains to this day.'

When Dubricius retired to the Island of Bardsey, David succeeded him as Bishop of Caerleon. However, he removed the seat of his bishopric from the busy city on the banks of the Usk to his own monastery of Menevia, which in after years was known by the name of its founder, the patron saint of Wales. Doubtless this step was taken on account of the advances made by the heathen Saxon. However, he frequently resided at Caerleon, and in 529 he convened a synod there which exterminated the Pelagian heresy, and has received the name of 'the Synod of Victory.' David appears to have been a hard-working prelate. Giraldus says, 'In his times, in Cambria, the Church of God flourished exceedingly, and ripened with much fruit every day. Monasteries were built everywhere; many congregations of the faithful of various orders were collected to celebrate with fervent devotion the sacrifice of Christ. But to all of them Father David, as if placed on a lofty eminence, was a mirror and pattern of life. He informed them by words, and he instructed them by example; as a preacher he was most powerful through his eloquence, but more so in his works.'

It is unfortunate that the memory of this great bishop is obscured by fantastic legends. The results of his unwearying labours still live, and although some details of his life are hidden in uncertainty, yet we cannot over-estimate the importance of the work he performed.

Samson, a son of Caw, was also educated in the schools of Illtyd. In after years he was consecrated a bishop; and legendary writers assert that he became Archbishop of York, but when the Saxons took the city and destroyed his cathedral he fled to Armorica.

Paulinus, or Paul Hên, was a native of North Britain. He, too, was a Llantwit student, and became a man of some note. He founded a school at Whitland in Carmarthenshire, and his fame as a teacher drew to him many students. David, as we have already seen, studied with him for ten years, and Teilo was one of his scholars. The name of Paul Hên is preserved in Capel Peulin, near Llanddewi Brefi. At Pant-y-Polion a stone* used to stand which was supposed to mark his grave. The inscription, written in bad Latin verse, may be expressed: 'One who kept the faith, and ever loved his country, Here Paulinus lies, a most pious observer of justice.'

The sons of chieftains from the north,† as well

---

* The stone is now kept on the estate of Dolan Cothi.

† Gwenddolen, Cor, and Nudd, sons of a northern chief; Amwn Ddu, son of Emyr Llydaw, an Armorican prince; Alan, another brother; Llenddad, Llonio Lawhir, and

as sons of Armorican princes, were sent to Llantwit for instruction. Some of these men are known to have studied elsewhere; whence we may suppose it was not an unusual practice to migrate from one college to another.

Padarn,* Pedrwn, or Paternus, as he is called in Latin, came to Britain about the year 516.† After his arrival in Wales he became a member of the college of St. Illtyd.‡ He afterwards established a religious society§ at a place in Cardiganshire, called in after times Llanbadarn Fawr (St. Padarn's Church the Greater), where he also founded an episcopal see, of which he became the

---

Llynab, sons of Alan; Eigrad and Peirio were sons of Cor and brother to Samson, who tradition says became Archbishop of York; Selyr, Cyngar, Jestin, and Cado, the sons of Geraint ab Erbin; Teon, and his son Tegonwy; Tathan, a son of Amwn Dhu, and brother of St. Samson of Dol; Isan; Mengan, son of Gwyndav Hen; Cawrdav, son of Caradog Vreichvras; Usteg, the son of Geraint ab Carannog, who was dean of the college; and his brother Eldad; and Eldad, the son of Arth.

* There is a 'Life of St. Padarn' by John of Tynemouth, and a Latin metrical 'Life' by John, son of Sulgen, who was Bishop of St. David's in 1070.

† According to Usher.

‡ Achan y Saint.

§ The Welsh accounts say it consisted of 120 members; John of Tynemouth declares that this institution contained 847 monks, who came with Padarn from Armorica. (See Rees' 'Essay,' pp. 216, 261; Usher's 'Britan. Eccles. Antiq.,' p. 275.)

ANCIENT FONT (LLANTWIT MAJOR).

first bishop.* From Johannes Sulgenus we learn that Padarn presided over this see for twenty-one years, during which time he spent his life in prayer, tears, fasting, hospitality, and attendance on the sick; and he is styled in the 'Triads' one of the three blessed visitors of the Isle of Britain. The others were Dewi (St. David) and Teilo. 'They were so called because they went as guests to the houses of the noble, the plebeian, the native, and the stranger, without accepting either fee or reward, or victuals or drink; but what they did was to teach the faith in Christ to everyone without pay or thanks. Besides which they gave to the poor and needy gifts of their gold and silver, their raiment and provisions.'†

The history of St. Padarn is obscure. He appears to have built monasteries and churches throughout Ceretica, and to have rebuked Maelgwn Gwynedd. When 'the great tempter of the saints,' as this powerful king was called, met Padarn, he met holiness, gentleness, love, and moral power, and for a moment the wild beast within him shrank, and he felt the awful power of goodness. Would that a lasting impression had

---

* This bishopric is mentioned in the Welsh chronicles in the year 720; and it has been thought that it was incorporated with St. David's in consequence of the murder of Idnerth, the last of its bishops.

† 'Triad' 19.

been made. It was hard for a man of that age to keep his Christianity if he did not become a monk, and if we understand the story of Maelgwn Gwynedd and Padarn aright, we shall have learnt to understand some of the problems which beset Celtic Christianity in the sixth century.

Padarn is said to have visited Ireland and then returned to Armorica, where he became Bishop of Vannes.* He subscribed the decrees of the Council of Paris held in 557, and is mentioned in the writings of Venantius Fortunatus, a Latin poet of Gaul, who was his contemporary.

The name of Madog Morvryn† occurs as a

---

* Called Guenet in the legend. There is some confusion with the name of Padarn. There were two Bishops of Vannes named Paternus, and a Bishop of Avranches of the same name. When at Vannes, Padarn is said to have been summoned by Samson, Archbishop of Dôl, at the instigation of a monk. St. Samson sent for him to come in whatever state he should be found to prove his humility. The story adds that Padarn repaired to him with a boot and stocking on one leg, and the other naked; and it also adds that the malicious monk was seized by a demon, and only released through the intercession of the good Bishop of Vannes.

† Madog Morvryn, according to 'Triad' 98, was one of 'the three blessed youth-trainers of the Isle of Britain.' He was also a bard. His son was Merddin Wyllt, and we subjoin an interesting dialogue, supposed to have passed between him and Columba of Iona.

'Black is thy steed, and black thy cap,
Black thy pate, thy head and all—
Art thou Colum?

teacher at Llantwit, and Gwyndav Hen appears to have been a chaplain until he was appointed head of the College at Caerleon.* His son, Meugan, was a student at Llantwit, and afterwards at Caerleon. Two of his poems are inserted in the Myvyrian Archæology.†

Some writers have given the names of Taliesin, and also Talhaiarn in their lists of Llantwit students. These great bards, however, are more intimately associated with Cadoc than with

> I am Colum the scholar,
> Of Scottish race, and fickle wit.
> Woe to him who drowns not the insulter of his sovereign.
>
> I burnt a church, and intercepted the kine of a monastery,
> And immersed in water the Sacred Book ;
> Wherefore I suffer a heavy penance.
>
> Creator of all creatures,
> Thou supreme supporter,
> Blot out for me mine iniquity.
>
> A full year have I been destined to occupy
> The post of a wear at Bangor :
> Behold thou the pain I have borne from sea animals.
>
> If I had known before what I now do know,
> How freely the wind whirls through the lofty branches,
> Never would I have committed the deed.'

Columba had a white horse, which used to carry the milk vessels between his monastery and the fold. Hence the question asked in the first verse.

* This college was founded by Dubricius, and according to some copies of Geoffrey of Monmouth, it contained two hundred philosophers, who studied astronomy and other sciences.

† Vol. i., pp. 159, 160.

Illtyd. It is not unlikely, however, that they may have studied at Bangor Illtyd for a short time.

The three sons of Alan, an Armorican prince, were educated at Bangor Illtyd. Lleuddad, the eldest, became Abbot of Bardsey, after Cadfan's death. There are poems extant which speak of the protection he afforded to pilgrims crossing to that sacred isle. Llonio Lawhir was dean of the college at Llanbadarn Fawr, while the third son, Llynab, retired to Bardsey. The statement in Achan y Saint, that he was Archbishop of Llandaff, seems to be incorrect.

Peirio, a son of Caw, became principal on the death of Illtyd, but he died on the following day, and was succeeded by Samson, son of Amwn Ddu. Another son of Amwn Ddu was also at Llantwit. His name was Tathan, and he founded the Church of St. Athan. He became the first principal of the college at Caerwent, in Monmouthshire, where he is said to have taught the liberal arts and sciences to a great number of scholars, who flocked to him from all parts of the country.

Before closing our list of names of men connected with Bangor Illtyd,* we must not forget Elphin, the son of Gwyddno, who was educated

* An old parchment is mentioned by Dr. Nichol ('Horæ Britannicæ,' vol. ii., p. 355) in which appear the names of

at Llantwit. The well-known legend relates how Gwyddno had a valuable weir at Aberdovey. It was usual to find in the weir the value of a hundred pounds on the 1st of May; and as a last resource Gwyddno gave Elphin, who was the most unlucky of men, the profits of the weir for one whole year. At the proper time, Elphin and his companions visited the weir, and their disappointment was great when they found nothing more valuable in it than a leathern bag. 'However,' remarked Elphin, 'this may contain the value of a hundred pounds.' The man who opened the bag exclaimed, on beholding a child's forehead, 'Here is a charming forehead (tal iessin)!' '*Taliessin** let him be,' said Elphin, as he lifted up the boy and bewailed his lack of luck. Presently the child sang a poem to console him.†
Elphin mounted his steed, and carried the child to his wife, who nursed the little one tenderly. From that hour Elphin's wealth increased. Such is the ancient story of the discovery of the chief

---

the principals of Llan Illtyd: Iltutus, Piro, Ivanus, Cennit, Samson, Gourthaver, Congers, Elbod, Tomre, Gurhavel, Nudh, Eliver, Segin, Camelauc, Bletri, and many more that cannot be read. It is observable that some of the foregoing were raised to the episcopacy, and were eminent men in their days.

* *Tàl iessin* means 'fine forehead;' and *Tàl iessin*, 'fine pay.' (See 'Guest,' iii., 328, 363.)

† 'The Consolation of Elphin.'

bard of Wales, committed by his mother to the chances of the tide, and found by the luckless Elphin. In after days, Elphin was imprisoned in the Castle of Dyganwy, and Taliesin, through the influence of his song, procured his release.

There appears to have been no appointed age at which members were admitted to the schools at Llantwit. Boys like St. Samson were sent there for instruction, and old men like Cawrdaf* passed the remainder of their days devoting their time to religious exercises. The world around had no pleasures to offer those who sought peace and holiness; and thus we see gathered together at Llantwit, youths who were receiving their education, and those who had returned to find a haven of refuge.

Scholars and bards, historians and poets, zealous missionaries and dignified ecclesiastics received their education at Llantwit; and we may venture to say that when barbarism was not yet extinct, when civil feuds were frequent, when passions were rife, when heresies beset the faithful, Llantwit exercised a wonderful influence, civilizing and teaching the people of Britain and Armorica.

* Cawrdaf was a sovereign in Brecknockshire, and is distinguished in 'Triad' 41, Third Series, for his extensive influence, for whenever he went to battle, the whole population of the country attended to his summons.

CHAPTER VII

HEATHENDOM

CHAPTER VII.

HEATHENDOM.

IT may be well, in this chapter, to give a sketch of the heathenism which confronted the Silurian Christians during and immediately after the Roman occupation. Long after the Christian faith had diffused itself through the life of the people, fragments of Celtic paganism were found woven into their literature, and may even now be met with in their folk-lore.

Numerous altars, dedicated to the gods of Rome, have been found, and others have been discovered erected in honour of foreign deities, worshipped by foreign soldiers, who formed the legionary cohorts. Sometimes the names of several gods and goddesses are grouped together on one altar; and occasionally the name of a local god is coupled with some divinity known to the Roman Pantheon.* Gildas, who wrote his

---

* At Bath altars were dedicated to Sul and Sul-Minerva. (See 'Roman Britain,' by Rev. H. M. Scarth, p. 190.)

celebrated history about the year 550, speaks of the grim-faced idols which stood in his day on the mouldering city walls.

A sanctuary of the god Nodens was discovered some years ago on hilly ground in Lydney Park, near the tidal bed of the Severn.* This Silurian god was not only a Mars, for the remains discovered in his temple lead us to believe that he was a kind of Neptune. On a mosaic floor are found representations of sea-serpents, fishes supposed to be salmon from the Severn, and a funnel-like hole, which was doubtless used for libations to Nodens. A plaque of bronze was discovered, and this shows the youthful god crowned with rays, and standing in a chariot drawn by four horses. Winged genii, typifying the winds, float on either side, and two Tritons are also represented. On a detached piece is another Triton, and also a fisherman who has hooked a salmon. This temple on the western bank of the Severn was built in Roman times, but doubtless the god was worshipped on this spot long before Julius Cæsar crossed over from Portus Itius.† In Welsh we find for Nodens the two forms Nûdd and Llûdd. One of the Welsh

---

* See 'Transactions of Bristol and Gloucester Archæological Society,' vol. vi., p. 1.

† One inscription found at Lydney calls him *Devo Nodenti*, another reads *D. M. Nodenti*, and a third *Deo Nudente M.*

names for London is Caer Lûdd, or Lud's Fort, and in that great city is still found the name of *Ludgate* Hill. 'The probability is,' says Professor Rhys,* 'that as a temple on the hill near the Severn associated him with that river in the west, so a still more ambitious temple on a hill connected him with the Thames in the east; and as an aggressive creed can hardly signalize its conquests more effectively than by appropriating the fanes of the retreating faith, no site could be guessed with more probability to have been sacred to the Celtic Zeus than the eminence on which the dome of St. Paul's now rears its magnificent form.'

It has been thought that the Zeus of Brythonic paganism may be traced in the stories which surround the name of Merlin Emrys—the king, the warrior, and the magician. One legend sends him to sea in a glass house, never more to be heard of, another places him in the haze of Bardsey, another leaves him bound by spells of his own magic in an impenetrable forest, whilst a Breton story gives him a tomb within a tree. 'These pictures,' says the learned Professor of Celtic in the University of Oxford, 'vie with one another in transparent truthfulness to the original scene in nature, with the sun as a centre of a vast expanse of light, which moves with him as he

* See 'Celtic Heathendom,' p. 129.

hastens towards the west. Even when at length one saw Merlin but a magician, and in his pellucid prison but a work of magic, the answer to the question, what had become of him and it, continued to be one which the store-house of nature-myths had supplied. Where could Merlin have gone but whither the sun goes to rest at night, into the dark sea, into an isle surrounded by the waves of the west, or into the dusk of an impenetrable forest?'*

The Druids were priests, medicine-men, and the instructors of the young. Judicial power seems to have been lodged with them, and they taught that the souls of men were incorruptible, and passed from one body to another, and they held that people were thereby most strongly urged to bravery, as the fear of death is thus destroyed. The oak-tree was specially sacred among the Druids. In oak groves they frequently performed their rites, and many have even derived their name from this custom. Now it is interesting to note that the oak appears to have been associated with the supreme god of the Aryans, and in early Greece the oak was symbolic of him. Pliny's well-known account of the Druids† is so much to the point that we trust we may be pardoned in quoting it at full length. 'Nor is the

* 'Celtic Heathendom,' p. 158.
† 'Natural History,' xvi., 95.

NINTH CENTURY CROSS IN THE WESTERN CHURCH
(LLANTWIT MAJOR).

admiration of Gaulish lands in this matter to be passed over in silence: the Druids, for so they call their magicians, have nothing which they hold more sacred than the mistletoe and the tree on which it grows, provided only it be an oak [*robur*]. But apart from that, they select groves of oak, and they perform no sacred rite without leaves from that tree, so that the Druids may be regarded as even deriving from it their name interpreted as Greek. For they believe whatever grows on these trees to be actually sent from heaven, and to form a mark in each instance of a tree selected by the god himself. That is, however, very rarely to be met with, and when it is found it is sought with much religious ceremony. They do this especially at the time of the sixth moon, the luminary which marks the beginning of their months and their years, and after the tree had passed the thirtieth year of its age, because of its having even then plenty of vigour, though not half the size to which it may grow. Addressing it in their language as the universal healer, and taking care to have sacrifices and banquets prepared with the correct ceremony beneath the tree, they bring to the spot two white bulls, whose horns have never been bound before. The priest, clad in a white robe, climbs the tree, and with a golden sickle cuts the mistletoe; it is caught in a white cloth. Then at length they sacrifice the victims, with a prayer that God may make His own gift benefit those to whom He has given it. They believe that drinking of a potion prepared from it gives fecundity to barren animals, and that it is a remedy against all poison.'

In Mâth,* Professor Rhys is of opinion, we may recognise the Welsh counterpart of the Goidelic god of Druidism. He could hear without regard to distance every sound of speech that reached the air, and he is named the first of the three great magicians of Welsh mythology, in which respect he may be compared to Merlin. He taught his arts to Gwydion,† with whose help he created a woman out of flowers. Mâth, unlike Zeus, is free from all feelings of jealousy or revenge. His justice is proverbial, and 'he may be distinctly pronounced the highest ideal, as regards the sense of justice and equity, that can be associated with the heathen element in Welsh literature.'‡

Mention has already been made of Gwydion, and he is described by Lucian under the Gaulish name of Ogmios,§ being the god of eloquence and

---

* Mâth ab Mathonwy, also called Mâth Hên, or M. the Ancient.
† Gwydion ab Dôn, the Culture Hero.
‡ 'Celtic Heathendom,' p. 226.
§ The Celtic Mercury.

all wisdom appertaining thereto. He acquired gifts of poetry and music from the nether world, and his favourite disguise was to take the form of a bard. He procured* animals useful for man, such as the dog and the pig, and he and his friends harry Hades, and secure the mystic cauldron out of which voices issued, and the inspiration of wisdom and poetry.

Llew, the sun-god, was Gwydion's son, and his wife,† we have already mentioned, was a creation by Gwydion and Mâth out of flowers, which may be a personification of dawn and the gloaming. One day when Llew was away a stranger visited his wife, and with him she compassed her husband's death. Gwydion, however, brought him back to life again, but the wretched woman fled before Gwydion, until her maidens fell into a lake, and she was herself converted into an owl by the touch of Gwydion's wand. Another story‡ tells us that Gwydion chased her across the heavens, and the Milky Way indicates his path.

Students of mythology have traced many points of similarity between Gwydion and Woden, and even between Gwydion - Woden and Indra. 'Above all,' says the author of 'Celtic Heathen-

---

* Gwydion procures them from his brother Amaethon, the farmer.
† Blodeuedd.
‡ See Morris' 'Celtic Remains,' p. 231.

dom,' 'one has to bear in mind the distortion which the Hindu side of the picture has undergone in consequence of the removal of the abode of the dead from the nether world to the most distant heaven. But when it is considered what a far cry it is from the shores of the Baltic to the land of the Five Rivers, how long it must have taken our kindred to reach it, and how largely their blood had by that time been mixed with that of other races, it is a matter of surprise that Sanskrit literature yields so many points of contact between Indra and Gwydion-Woden.'

In the story of Llûdd* we read of a race of dwarfs,† who were able to hear every sound of speech that reached the air. Llûdd invited them to a banquet, together with his own people, and he then besprinkled them with water, in which a certain insect had been ground. This killed these hideous and most mischievous creatures,‡ without harming anyone else. Besides destroying the dwarfs, Llûdd overcame the thieving giant who spread siren music around him, and who carried away Llûdd's feasts in a basket that was never full.§

* R. B. Mab., p. 96 ; Guest, iii., 311.
† These dwarfs were called ' Coranians.'
‡ These dwarfs correspond to the Irish Luchorpáin.
§ Professor Rhys is of opinion that this giant survives in Welsh nurseries under the name of *Siôn y Cydau*, or Jack with the Bags.

Beside malignant dwarfs and thieving giants, there were Celtic fairies, which are undoubtedly relics of those *matres* and *matronæ* which appear in Gallo-Roman inscriptions as objects of popular belief. The fairies were supposed to be only a few inches high, almost transparent in body, so airy that they could dance on dew-drops with foxglove flowers for head-dresses, and robes made of thistledown. No mortal could compare with their exquisite beauty, and their societies were governed by a lovely queen. Although they could not be seen they were believed to be ever present, and could hear all that was said. So men spoke of them respectfully, and called them ' the good folk.' They were believed to make their homes in the crevices of the rock or in the ancient tumuli, and the small arrow-heads of prehistoric men were supposed to be used by these 'little good folk,' but not always with the kindest intentions, for if a poor man's heifer was suddenly afflicted, it was said to be their work. Every portion of their tiny homes was splendidly decorated, and those who have been so fortunate as to hear sweet music float on the midnight air, believed it came from their fairy palaces. They had their rings,* their merry

* The fairy-rings are now known to be due to the outwardly spreading growth of the perennial subterranean mycelium of various fungi, chiefly species of Agaricus.

meetings, and their gifts, and they occasionally stole a child from its cradle. But usually these tiny, ever busy, frolicsome creatures befriended the sorrowful and the oppressed, and rewarded their friends.

Holy wells date from prehistoric times, and there is little doubt that many of them have been venerated in a remote past. Water-worship was common to ancient paganism. Water was considered a living being, and possessed powers which could bring a blessing on the worshippers, or could destroy their property and prosperity. Consequently wells and streams received worship, and offerings were made to them either from fear or out of gratitude.

The wells still remain under a form of guardianship which in the minds of many people bears connection with ancient pagan priestcraft. In a paper which Professor Rhys wrote on 'The Folk-Lore of certain Sacred Wells in Wales,' he tells us that curative properties were attributed to the waters; but in one instance—that of St. Elian's—a certain ceremony was gone through at the well, in order to invoke curses upon the head of any person who might be objectionable to the devotee. A thriving business was formerly done by the owners or guardians of this place, for not only did they charge a sum of money for inscribing on a register the names of the persons to be cursed, but they reaped a harvest from the persons themselves, by exacting a fee for removing their names from the register. The water of St. Teilo's well was famous, Professor Rhys tells us, for whooping-cough. It was necessary, however, to take the water from the hand of a member of the Melchtor family, who were the guardians of the well, and to drink it out of St. Teilo's skull, which the family professed to hand round for the purpose.

If such ceremonies linger on into the nineteenth century, what must have been the strength of Celtic heathenism in the days of Dyfrig and Illtyd?

CHAPTER VIII

A UNIVERSITY TOWN

CHAPTER VIII.

A UNIVERSITY TOWN.

LET us rest awhile in the God's Acre at Llantwit Major, and as we throw ourselves upon the green turf, leaning against the shaft of Samson's cross, we will picture as best we can the Llanilltyd Fawr, as it existed at the end of the fifth century.

Here on the Glamorganshire coast, within sound of the sea which the affectionate Celt loved so well, were situated Illtyd's famous schools. They possessed no domes and stately towers like our Oxford and Cambridge, yet, nevertheless, this was a great seat of learning at the end of the fifth and during the sixth century.

We hailed a student clad in his *cuculla* made of wool, of the natural colour of the material, beneath which we saw he had a white undergarment, called a *tunica;* and in his sociable companionship we passed the ditch and quadrangular wall, made of earth and stones, surrounding this university town. We found our youthful companion a good-natured fellow. We were soon on intimate terms, and his kindly heart, his love of nature, his gentleness to dumb animals, and his enthusiasm for his work and teachers won our affection. We explained we were strangers, and our young friend at once showed us the 'lions' of the place. He conducted us to Illtyd's Church. That oratory he consecrated after the Celtic custom,* by fasting and prayer during Lent—fasting each day until eventide, except on the Lord's Day. Even then he took nothing save a little bread, one egg, and a little milk and water. The church was of rude construction,† built of moorstone and round

* See account of the Celtic practice of consecrating churches given in Bede, 'H.E.,' iii., 23.

† There is little doubt that many of these Celtic churches were built of sawn timber and roofed with reeds. The stone church built on Eileann-na-Naoimb (see Appendix, p. 323, to Rees' 'Life of Columba,' by Adamnan), in which Columba consecrated the mysteries of the Holy Eucharist, and the stone church of St. Piran in Cornwall, lead us to believe that it was not unlikely that Illtyd's Church was built of stone. It may have taken the form of a basilica like the little building found at Silchester, and thought by some eminent authorities to have been a Christian church; or it may have been of a circular form, for Taliesin speaks of 'ecclesiæ rotundæ' (see 'Myv. Arch.,' v. i., 170). However, in this account we have preferred to follow the arrangement in the Church of St. Piran, which was built about this period, and

pebbles, taken from the banks of the stream, put together in the simplest way, and embedded in clay mortar. The doorway, which faced the south, had a plain moulding round it, with a carved head on the keystone, and one on each side of the spring of the arch. The windows were not large, and were filled with glass brought from a neighbouring Roman villa.* In the west

---

is still in existence, having been preserved by the sand through the long centuries. (See *Jour. Brit. Arch. Assoc.*, xlviii., p. 81.)

* In 1888 Mr. John Storrie discovered a Roman villa in a field locally known as Caermead, lying about a mile to the north-north-west of Llantwit Major. The excavation was only partial, and it is to be hoped that it may be resumed. The sites of several rooms were discovered. One room measured 60 feet by 51 feet. Mr. Storrie believed it to have been a prætorium. In some parts the walls were 9 feet high. Next to this room was a chamber, 12 feet square, which was perhaps a workshop, as many metallic fragments were found in it. To the south of this apartment was a large hall, 39 feet by 27 feet. It was divided into two compartments by a slight wall, pierced by a wide door space, most likely covered by curtains, easily removable. This room had a handsome tessellated pavement, and no fewer than forty-one human skeletons of both sexes and all ages were met with, as well as the bones of three horses. This hall was evidently the scene of a massacre, for, in nearly every instance, the skull or facial bones had been fractured, while the bodies lay in confused heaps. An attempt at burial had been made in four instances; the pavement had been torn up, and the body laid in an opening not more than six inches deep, its feet

wall was another doorway,* while attached to the building on one side was the sacristy where Illtyd's famous bell was kept which summoned the congregation to service. Our guide bid us enter this *sacra domus,* and we willingly followed him. We found the small building divided into chancel and nave, with a screen separating them, while under the small east window stood the stone altar, with the *discus* and *calix* placed upon it. This fifth century church was rude in construction, simple in style, and possessed few

---

towards the east, and then surrounded with stones in the form of a coffin. Mr. W. E. Winks, in a paper sent to the *Athenæum* (October 20, 1888), says the unburied bodies belonged to a small race with brachycephalic skulls ; but those that were buried were clearly men of a larger size, and had skulls of the dolichocephalic type. Mr. Storrie surmises they were comrades of the victors who fell in the attack, while the unburied were the vanquished ; and he also suggests from the general absence of weapons, personal ornaments, and similar articles, that after these were plundered they were simply left to lie where they fell. After the villa was sacked it was burnt down, and pavements and bodies were buried under the débris. It has been conjectured that the massacre was perpetrated by Irish pirates in the fifth century A.D. For a list of the objects found, see a paper in *The Antiquary,* August, 1892, by Mr. John Ward, on 'Cardiff Museum.'

* The west doorway and the sacristy are not found at St. Piran's Church, but it appears to have been the arrangement at Iona and other Celtic churches. Mr. Skene gives a description of a Celtic monastery in 'Celtic Scotland,' ii., 59.

WESTERN LADY CHAPEL (LLANTWIT MAJOR).

architectural pretensions, yet here prayer and praise* ascended day and night without ceasing to the Giver of all. This was no glorious shrine, rich in storied windows or costly mosaics, like the chapels of King's College, Cambridge, or Keble's at Oxford; yet here the same Creed was recited, the same Faith preached, and the Holy Eucharist celebrated. Here members of the schools — warm-hearted Celtic youths—knelt side by side with older men who had come to Llantwit to find a haven of refuge away from the strife, anger, and jealousy of the heathen world around them.

Our youthful companion conducted us out of the oratory, and told us that the Holy Eucharist was called the 'Sacrifice,' that it was 'offered' by the priest, that the deacon could 'hold the chalice,'† and if a bishop were present he always celebrated.‡ He also told us that the Celtic

---

* 'Illtyd,' says one tradition, 'founded seven churches, and appointed seven companies for each church, and seven halls or colleges in each company, and seven saints in each hall or college, and prayer and praise were kept up without ceasing day and night, by twelve saints, men of learning, of each company.' Iolo MSS., p. 555. This perpetual service was called 'Laus perennis.'

† Canon XII., in 'Excerpta de Libro Davidis,' Haddan and Stubbs, i., 119.

‡ Adamnan in his biography of Columba says that on one occasion a bishop from Munster came, who through modesty concealed his office. At the celebration Columba discovered

Church possessed a liturgy, and that portions of the psalms were daily chanted, while lessons of the ordinal were taken from a variety of the old Latin version of the Bible* used prior to the Vulgate, as there was no Celtic translation.

The church we have just visited, although interesting as being the one built by Illtyd, was only one of seven oratories or 'college chapels,' as we should now call them. Near each was situated the so-called 'hall' or 'college'—a great wooden building built with joists. Not far from each 'college' was a refectory, also constructed of wood. Our young friend took us into the one where he was accustomed to dine at the long wooden table. He pointed out to us the ladles and strainers,† drinking-cups,‡ knives,§ wide but shallow spoons for eating the national dish of

---

that he was a bishop, and said, 'Christ bless thee, brother; do thou break bread alone, according to the episcopal rite; for I know now thou art a bishop. Why hast thou disguised thyself so long, and prevented our giving thee the honour due to thee?'

* On comparing quotations in Gildas, Fastidius, Columbanus, and other Celtic writers, we see there was a variety of the old Latin version. There appears to be no evidence of a Celtic translation.

† 'Vita Sancti Columbæ,' liber i., cap. xi

‡ *Ib.*, liber ii., cap. xxxiv.

Ib., liber ii., cap. xxx.

porridge,* made of bronze, with handles of the very shortest kind, earthenware pots,† having four handles, so that they could be easily drawn

* Celestius, an Irishman and follower of Pelagius, ran foul against St. Jerome, and the learned doctor of the Church tells him that he crams himself over much with Irish porridge: 'Nec intelligit (Celestius) Scotorum pultibus prægravatus' (S. Hieronimus in Prophetam Hieremian). 'Now reader,' says Mr. E. L. Barnwell, in his paper on 'Celtic Spoons' in the *Journal of the Archæological Institute*, 'just shadow forth to yourself this same Celestius and some friends seated at some meal, with, in their midst, an earthenware pot having four handles, so that it could be easily drawn to his own side by any individual guest, and you will see at once that while these spoons, by their shallow wideness, answered their every meal's purpose of cooling, at the will of him who had to sip from out of it, the portion he had ladled for himself from the seething mass, they at the same moment show us a passage of the everyday life of the Celts.' Some of these Celtic spoons appear to have been used for the service of the Christian Church, and have the sign of the cross on the bowl, or three circles on the handle—the sign of the Trinity. They are occasionally found in pairs, near springs of water or near some streamlet, and if found in pairs one has a small hole bored through it, just below the lip. It has been conjectured that such spoons were used for giving the sacrament of baptism—one for holding the oil of the catechumens, and the one with the hole in it for pouring out the oil of chrism. The Celts always preferred to use 'living water' for this rite. Hence these baptismal spoons are sometimes found in rivers or at springs. In some cases they may have been dropped accidentally and lost, or perhaps they have been left there on purpose.

† Such a pot was found on Portland Isle, and figured in the *Journal of the Archæological Institute*, vol. xxv.

to one side of the table or the other, and other furniture of a fifth century dining-hall. Passing out of the refectory we visited the kitchen with its utensils for cooking, such as bowls, jugs, water-pots,* frying-pans, and griddles. Our guide next pointed out two plain unpretentious wooden buildings, a little apart from the surrounding village, and he told us that one was the house of the Principal and the other was the guest-house. He then conducted us with considerable pride to a thatch-roofed house, which was nothing more nor less than the Bodleian of Bangor Illtyd. Here the books were preserved. We saw copies of various books of the Old and New Testament, ecclesiastical writers, and profane authors. On the tables stood other literary apparatus—the *tabulæ* or waxed tablets, the *graphia* or styles, the *calami* or pens, the *cornicula atramenti* or ink-horns—all ready for the work of the industrious scribe or the use of the diligent student. Upon the walls hung leathern cases, in which those books were kept that were occasionally taken away.†

We noticed multitudes of detached huts clustering round the various churches, 'colleges,' and refectories, and our young Celtic friend told us

* The *dabhach* was the water-pot of the Irish.

† Many of the above facts are extracted from 'Vita Sancti Columbæ auctore Adamnano.'

that these were the students' lodgings, or the cells of those who had joined the community more as monks than as students. These huts were of wattle and daub, and all were simple and humble. What would one of our gay undergraduates of Trinity, Cambridge, or Baliol, Oxford, think of such apartments? Our guide courteously showed us the one he occupied. He apologized for the untidiness of his room. An *amphibalus** and a *tunica* lay on the floor, while some shoes and sandals were carelessly placed on a wooden box. This was the only available seat in the room, and our host soon displaced the shoes and sandals to a more humble position, so that we might be seated. In one corner we noticed his bed; it was provided with a straw pallet and a pillow. We saw no coverlet, however, for our young friend slept in his ordinary clothes. His stock of books consisted of a roll of Psalms, and unlike Chaucer's undergraduate, he had not

> 'Twenty bookes, clothed in blak and reed,
> Of Aristotil and of his philosophie,'

but then, Chaucer's undergraduate lived some eight hundred years later, and even then he must have been quite a bibliophile. On the wall, arranged like a trophy, were his bow and arrows,

---

* The *amphibalus* was a warmer garment, and was worn instead of the *cuculla* when the weather required it.

a couple of daggers, and a short Roman sword, which the young student had bought from a Jew when he was last in Caerleon.

After a short rest we again set forth on our ramble. Our first visit was to the mills,* standing by the little river, and near them was the stone kiln for drying the corn. Our enthusiastic guide showed us the great barn where the grain when winnowed was stored in heaps.

Many students were busily engaged in work at the smithy and in the carpenter's shop. We passed outside the vallum and visited the *Bocetum* with its cows, and *lactaria vascula*, the *Prædium* with its horse and cart, and the *Pontus* with its craft of various sizes under the shadow of 'castle ditches.'

Near the meandering stream were the pasture lands, and in the fields around we saw some of the students busy at work receiving instruction in agriculture and husbandry.† Very practical indeed was the manner of teaching agriculture and

---

* The quern may have been the mill in use, although we read in the Iolo MSS., p. 420, the following: 'In 340 A.D. wind and water mills were first erected in Cambria, where previously only hand mills were known.'

† The course of instruction adopted by Illtyd embraced not only such sacred and profane literature as was requisite for a clerical education, but also included husbandry and other useful arts. (See 'Triad' 56; Williams' 'History of Monmouthshire,' Appendix, pp. 45-53.)

horticulture, and even at that date the name of Illtyd was a household word in connection with the plough. We saw a number of the younger boys driving the sparrows away from the corn,* while some of the older students were at work in the fields.† We were shown the beehives,‡ also the orchard with its rows of apple-trees.§ There were a few pear and cherry trees, apricot and quince, mulberry and fig, medlar and chestnut. These, our obliging guide told us, had been introduced into Britain by the Romans. We asked if there were any vines, and were informed that there were many vineyards on the southern slopes of the Silurian hills.‖ The flower garden delighted us,¶ and we were interested in noticing

* We read in the 'Liber Landavensis' that the boys in the school took it in turns to drive the sparrows away from the cornfields.

† 'Liber Landavensis.'

‡ Bees were kept, for we know that St. Samson and other Llantwit students kept them in Dol, and other settlements in Armorica.

§ Apple-trees were certainly cultivated, and when Glastonbury was called Avallonia, St. Samson took apple-trees to Dol; and it has already been mentioned that he and Telio planted an immense orchard, three miles in extent.

‖ The Romans planted vineyards on the Silurian hills.

¶ Flower gardens had been introduced into Britain by the Romans, and it is not unlikely there was one at Llantwit.

the artificial means adopted to increase the fertility of the soil.*

Before returning to the enclosure we climbed 'castle ditches,' and looked down on the great embankment which had been raised to prevent the waters of the Bristol Channel flooding the low-lying meadows.†

* * * * *

The sea, the brook, the fields remain, but the ditch, the stone wall, the oratories, the populous village of wooden huts, the 'halls,' the refectories, and the men and boys who peopled them have disappeared ages ago. Still, we are all members of the same family, moved by the same passions, influenced by the same affections; so let us stretch forth a hand of recognition over the centuries that intervene to those who lived, worked, and died in this time-honoured place.

* This is testified to as early as the time of Pliny, and even lime appears to have been used in some places for manure.

† 'Vita Sancti Iltuti,' xiii. (Ex. Coll. Lib. Britt. Mus. Vespasian, A., iv.).

CHAPTER IX
STUDY

CHAPTER IX.

STUDY.

WE sometimes fancy that we live in an age profoundly different from the time of Illtyd, and Dubricius, Cadoc, and Taliesin. We reflect on the various aspects of our complex civilization with a certain degree of complacency, and we regard our discoveries with self-satisfaction, forgetful that the past was the foundation of the present. Was not life then as full of joy and pleasure, sorrow, and agony, as it is to-day; and were not death and the hereafter as present to the men and women of the fifth century as they are to ourselves? Let us endeavour to look back over some fourteen centuries, and catch a glimpse of the study carried on at Llantwit Major, and perchance this slender setting forth of the past may help us to view tne present in a clearer light.

The young Celtic student was again our willing guide, and he first conducted us to one of the large wooden halls or 'colleges.' Here we found a number of students engaged in the study of the Holy Scriptures, which formed a prominent feature in the daily curriculum.*

In another portion of the large hall an aged teacher was dictating a number of the wise sayings attributed to Cadoc of Llancarfan, and the students grouped around were taking them down on their waxed tablets with their styles. As we approached we heard the old man saying:

'The three roots of all evil: falsehood, covetousness and pride.†

'The three contrasts of goodness: pride, anger, and covetousness.‡

---

* Gildas in his Epistle quotes from the following:—Old Testament: Genesis, Exodus, Deuteronomy, Samuel I. and II., Kings I. and II., Chronicles II., Job, Psalms, Proverbs, Ecclesiastes, Isaiah, Jeremiah, Lamentations, Ezekiel, Hosea, Joel, Amos, Micah, Habakkuk, Zephaniah, Haggai, Zechariah, Malachi. Apocrypha: Esdras, Ecclesiasticus, Wisdom. New Testament: St. Matthew, St. John, Acts, Romans, Corinthians I. and II., Galatians, Ephesians, Philippians, Colossians, Thessalonians I., Timothy I. and II., Titus, Hebrews, Peter I. and II. Gildas, when he was at Llancarfan, transcribed a copy of the four Gospels. (See 'Life of Gildas,' by Caradoc of Llancarfan.) He is supposed to have written the 'Book of St. Chad,' which consists at present of the Gospels of St. Matthew, St. Mark, and part of St. Luke to ch. iii., ver. 9. (See 'Liber Landavensis,' p. 615, note.) Taliesin appears also to have been well instructed in the historical events recorded in the Bible.

† 'Myv. Arch.,' vol. ii. ‡ *Ibid.*

GATE-HOUSE OF THE MEDIÆVAL MONASTERY
(LLANTWIT MAJOR).

'The three principal Divine qualities of man: liberality, love, and forgiveness of injuries.*
'The three principal good qualities of man: industry, sincerity, and humility.'†

We passed quietly on and found a smaller group of students, each with his waxed tablet before him, engaged in committing to memory that which had already been dictated. On one we saw the 'Triads of St. Paul,'‡ which we will venture to transcribe.

'1. There are three sorts of men: the man of God, who renders good for evil; the man of man, who renders good for good, and evil for evil; and the man of the devil, who renders evil for evil.

'2. Three sorts of people are the delight of God: the meek; the lovers of peace; and the lovers of mercy.

'3. There are three marks of the children of God: humble demeanour; a pure conscience; and the suffering of injuries patiently.

---

* 'Myv. Arch.,' vol. iii., p. 77.

† *Ibid.*

‡ The learned author of 'The Ecclesiastical Antiquities of the Cymry' says that these aphorisms appear, by their title, style, and form to have been of the earliest date, and they may accordingly be considered as the homiletic remains of the Cambrian Church, whilst it was yet in connection with bardism.

'4. The three principal things required of God: love, justice, and humility.

'5. In three places will be found the most of God: where He is mostly sought; where mostly loved; and where there is the least of self.

'6. There are three sorts of lies: verbal lies; the lies of silence; and the lies of false appearances; each inducing us to believe what we should not.

'7. Three things shall a man obtain by a belief in God: what is necessary in this life; a peaceable conscience; and communion with heaven.

'8. The three advices given by Lazarus are: "Believe in God, who made thee; love God, who redeemed thee; and fear God, who will judge thee."

'9. Three ways a Christian punishes an enemy: by forgiving him; by not divulging his wickedness; and by doing him all the good that is possible.

'10. The three great concerns of a Christian: lest he should offend God; lest he should be a stumbling-block to man; and lest his love towards all that is good should fail.

'11. The three evidences of holiness: self-denial; a liberal disposition; and the encouragement of all that is good.

'12. The three dainties of Christian festivity: what God has prepared; what can be obtained consistently with justice to all; and what love to all can venture to use.

'13. Three persons have the claims and privileges of brothers and sisters: the orphan; the widow; and the alien.'

On another tablet we saw the 'Counsels of Cadoc to King Arawn.'

'Turn a deaf ear to every bad language;
Turn thy back to every bad deed;
Turn a closed eye to every thing monstrous;
Turn thy sight and heart to everything beautiful;
Turn thy open hand to every poverty;
Turn thy mind to every generosity;
Turn thy reason to the counsels of the wise;
Turn thy affection to things Divine;
Turn thy devotion to every goodness;
Turn thy whole genius with a view to excel;
Turn thy understanding to know thyself;
Turn all thy sciences to accord with nature;
Turn all thy faculties upon what is happy:
Turn all thy heart and might upon God the Lord.'*

On a third tablet we read these wise words:

'Consider before thou speakest,
First, what thou speakest;
Secondly, why thou speakest;
Thirdly, to whom thou speakest;

* 'Myv. Arch.,' vol. iii., p. 58.

Fourthly, concerning whom thou speakest;
Fifthly, what will come of what thou speakest;
Sixthly, what will be the benefit of what thou speakest;
Seventhly, who may be listening to what thou speakest.
Place thy word on the end of thy finger before thou speakest it,
And turn it there seven ways before thou speakest it,
And no harm will ever result from what thou speakest.'*

While on a fourth we read a plain moral truth:

'There is no man a hero save him that will speak the truth.
There is nothing near a man save what he cannot reach himself.
There is no loud voice save that which no one hears—conscience.
No man has sense save him that perceives he is a fool.
There is no man thoughtful save him that is quiet.'

We left the hall as quietly as we had entered it, and as we passed the library we saw the librarian

---

* 'Myv. Arch.,' vol. iii.

busily occupied in teaching the art of writing and the illumination of manuscripts, which was brought to a high state of perfection by these Celtic students. One was making a copy of St. Patrick's grand song—the 'Coat of Mail.' He had just copied the words:

'Christ with me, Christ before me,
Christ behind me, Christ within me,
Christ beneath me, Christ above me,
Christ on my right, Christ on my left,
Christ in the fort,
Christ in the chariot-seat,
Christ in the poop,

Christ in the heart of every man who thinks of me,
Christ in the mouth of every man who speaks to me,
Christ in every eye that sees me,
Christ in every ear that hears me.'

Some students were reading volumes that had been lent to them, and we noticed that one was absorbed in the perusal of Virgil.*

* It is narrated that Virgil was Cadoc's favourite author, and he made his scholars learn his writings by heart. The following charming story is told of him. 'One day, while walking with his friend and companion, the famous historian Gildas, with his Virgil under his arm, the Abbot began to weep at the thought that the poet whom he loved so much

Our guide showed us the boys' school, and we saw a number of bright little fellows learning the Articles of the Creed, while others were committing to memory 'The Ages of the World.'

'The first was the age of Adam and Eve;
The second, the age of Noah, who floated in the ark;
The third age was that of Abraham, the chief of the faithful, the father of patriarchs;
The fourth, the age of Moses from Egypt,
Who discovered the twelve ways through the Red Sea,
Who obtained of the invisible God that Pharaoh should be drowned,
Who during his fasting received the ten commandments,
On two tables of stone, on Mount Sinai;

---

might be even then perhaps in hell. At the moment when Gildas reprimanded him severely for that *perhaps*, protesting that without any doubt Virgil must be damned, a sudden gust of wind tossed Cadoc's book into the sea. He was much moved by this accident, and, returning to his cell, said to himself, "I will not eat a mouthful of bread nor drink a drop of water before I know truly what fate God has allotted to those who sang upon earth as the angels sing in heaven." After this he fell asleep, and soon after, dreaming, heard a soft voice addressing him. "Pray for me," said the voice; "never be weary of praying; I shall yet sing eternally the mercy of the Lord."' The next day the book which he had lost was restored in a wonderful way. (See Montalembert, 'Monks of the West,' bk. viii., ch. ii.)

The fifth age, the age of Jesus, and it will endure until the day of doom.'*

We noticed that one end of the schoolroom was a plastered wall, upon which a map was painted for the study of geography.†

Our young friends would not be sorry when their lessons were finished, and they were free to bound over the green-sward in the meadows, under the shadow of 'Castle Ditches,' or ramble on the coast and fling pebbles over the arch in Trysillion's wave-washed cavern.

We were next conducted to another hall, where was a white-haired philosopher, clad in his linen robe of pure white, one side folded over the other, and fastened by a loop and button at the shoulder. His sleeves were open on the upper side, showing the white tunic underneath, with its tight-fitting sleeves and cuffs turned up at the wrists and cut in points.‡ Students of various ages surrounded

---

* 'Myv. Arch.,' vol. i., p. 96. Nennius enumerates them thus: The first, from Adam to Noah; the second, from Noah to Abraham; the third, from Abraham to David; the fourth, from David to Daniel; the fifth, from Daniel to St. John the Baptist; the sixth, from St. John the Baptist to the Day of Judgment. ('Hist. Brit.,' sec. 6.)

† The Romans had maps painted on walls, and this method of teaching geography was doubtless in use at Llantwit Major, for the Bovium of the Romans was in the immediate neighbourhood of Illtyd's schools.

‡ James, 'Patriarchal Religion of Britain,' p. 75.

this venerable professor, and we saw the styles move over the waxen tablets as the old man exclaimed:

'There are three kinds of stars: fixed stars, which keep their places, and are called stationary stars; erratic stars, which are called planets,* of which there are fifteen, seven being continually visible, and eight invisible, except very seldom from their moving within the galaxy and beyond it; and the third are irregular stars, which are called comets, and nothing is known of their place, number, or time, nor are they themselves known except on occasions of chance, and in the cycle of ages.'†

Our youthful guide found little interest in the professor's discourse, and beckoned us to follow him. We were loath to leave, for we knew that the names of thirty-seven constellations‡ had

---

* Taliesin says: 'The planets are seven—Sola, Luna, Marcarucia, Venerus, Severus, Jupiter, and Saturnus.'

† Llandover MS.

‡ *Caer Arianrod*, the circle of Arianrod; *yr Orsedd wen*, the white throne; *Telyn Arthur*, Arthur's harp; *Caer Gwydion*, the circle of Gwydion; *yr Haeddel fawr*, the plough tail; *yr Haeddel fach*, the smaller plough handle; *y Llong fawr*, the great ship; *y Llong foel*, the bald ship; *y Llatheidan*, the yard; *y Twr Tewdws*, Theodosius's group; *y Tryfelan*, the Triangle; *Llys Don*, the circle of Don; *Llwyn Blodenwedd*, the grove of Blodenwedd; *Cadair Teyrnon*, the chair of Teyrnon; *Caer Eiddionydd*, the circle of Eiddionydd; *Caer Sidi*, the circle of Sidi; *Cwlwm cancaer*,

THIRTEENTH-CENTURY PIGEON-HOUSE
(LLANTWIT MAJOR).

been handed down, and we wished to hear the professor's remarks on the knowledge of Hipparchus of Bithynia—the theorist, the mathematician, and the observer. This Asiatic sage had catalogued more than a thousand stars, discovered the precession of the equinoxes and the eccentricity of the sun's path, determined the length of the solar year and the distances of the sun and moon respectively from the earth, and invented the planisphere. We wished to hear his remarks on the teaching of Ptolemy, whose most important discovery was the evection of the moon, and who was the first to point out atmospheric refraction. However, we gathered that the professor considered with Ptolemy that the earth was immovable in the centre of the universe, making the entire heavens revolve round it in the course of twenty-four hours.

---

the conjunction of a hundred circles; *Ll'uest Elmur*, the camp of Elmur; *Bwa'r Milwr*, the soldier's bow; *Bryn Dinan*, the hill of Dinan; *Nyth yr Eryres*, the eagle's nest; *Trosol Bleiddyd*, Bleiddyd's lever; *Asgell y gwynt*, the wind's wing; *y Feillionen*, the trefoil; *Pair Cariadwen*, the cauldron of Caridwen; *Dolen Teifi*, the bend of Teivi; *yr Esgair fawr*, the great limb; *yr Esgair fechan*, the small limb; *yr Ychen bannog*, the large-horned oxen; *y Maes mawr*, the great plain; *y Fforch wen*, the white fork; *y Baedd coed*, the woodland boar; *Llywethan*, the muscle; *yr Hebog*, the hawk; *March Llyr*, the horse of Llyr; *Cadair Elffin*, Elffin's chair; *Neuadd Olwen*, Olwen's hall. (See Llandover MS.)

We gathered also from what the venerable philosopher was saying that the *via lactea* or the 'Milky Way' was known by the name of Gwydion,* the 'Northern Crown' was the 'Circle of Arianrod,' and the 'Lyre' was 'Arthur's harp.' The 'Great Bear' was the 'Plough tail,' 'Orion' was the 'Yard,' the 'Pleiades' was 'Theodosius's group,' and 'Cassiopeia's chair' was the 'circle of Don.' The 'ecliptic' and the 'twins' we also discovered were respectively known as the 'circle of Sidi' and the 'large-horned oxen.'

We passed a class where instruction in weaving† and knitting was being given, and we hastened to

---

* 'The three blessed astronomers of the Isle of Britain: Idris Gawr; Gwydion, son of Don; and Gwyn, son of Nudd. So great was their knowledge of the stars, and of their nature and situation, that they could foretell whatever might be desired to be known, to the day of doom.' ('Triad' 89, Third Series.) At an early period the science of astronomy (*seryddiaeth*) was studied by the Cymry, and it has been pointed out that (see Williams' 'Traditionary Annals of the Cymry,' p. 247) one of the oldest words which has been, and still is, used to denote time is Amser, which literally signifies the revolution of the stars. There seems little doubt that astronomy was taught at Llantwit Major, for Geoffrey of Monmouth says it was studied at St. Dubricius' School at Caerleon, where Meugan, son of Gwyndar Hên, the president, worked for some time after leaving Bangor Illtyd.

† *Gwehyddiaeth* is very ancient. In the code of Dyvnwal Moelmud it is stated: 'There are three domestic arts, being primary branches—husbandry, or cultivation of the

the end of the hall, attracted by the sound of music.* Here a teacher was instructing his class in the art of playing the harp or Telyn.† It was strung with horse's hair, and had only one row of strings, and no mechanism whatever for the production of sharps or flats, or of modulating from the key in which the instrument was tuned.‡

---

land; pastoral care; and weaving; and the chiefs of kindreds are to enforce instruction in them, and to answer in that respect in court, and in village, and in every assembly for worship.' (See 'Welsh Laws and Institutions,' ii., p. 515.) In 1838 an interesting specimen of the herring-bone pattern, and which appears to have been a sleeve, was discovered in a stone cist near Micklegate Bar, York; while in 1786, in a bog in the county of Longford, another specimen of ancient British manufacture was discovered. This is described as 'a woollen coat of coarse, but even network, exactly in the form of what is now called a spencer.'

* Tydain Tad Awen is said first to have reduced music to a system or art.

† From *telu*, to stretch or strain.

‡ The Venerable Bede tells us that in the seventh century the harp was so generally played in Britain that it was customary to hand it from one to another at their entertainments, and mentions one who, ashamed that he could not play upon it, slunk away lest he should expose his ignorance. Mr. John Thomas (Harpist to the Queen) mentions in the February number of the *Victorian Magazine* that the harp was held in such honour in Wales that a slave might not practise it; that to be able to play upon it was an indispensable qualification of a gentleman, and that it could not be taken for debt. A professor of this favourite instrument enjoyed many privileges; his lands were free and his person

We left the aged astronomer, the musician, and the teacher of the art of weaving, and passed into another hall. Our guide did not allow us to linger long beside a group of students seated near the entrance. They were being instructed in the art of pleading, for the office of an advocate in ancient days was very similar to that of a barrister, or counsellor learned in the law, in our own times. The jurist had been illustrating some point from the famous Moelmutian code, and was saying: ' A law advocate, who shall be an advocate between a Cymro and an alien ignorant of the language . . . has the privilege of his five acres under the privilege and protection of his art, independently

---

sacred. An old manuscript, transcribed by Robert ab Huw, in the time of Charles I., from a still older document, has elements in it which may be traced to early times. Some of the directions are as follows : ' The 6th tune is played as the 5th, only raising two notes on the upper thumb. The 12th is played like the 10th, only shaking the upper thumb. The 14th is played like the 13th, but raising three notes on the upper thumb.' The following curious terms are used : ' Choaking the thumb ;' ' shake of the four fingers,' evidently a double shake ; 'shake of the little finger,' not used now ; 'double scrape,' probably drawing two fingers along the strings in thirds or sixes ; ' single scrape ;' 'half scrape ;' ' throw of the finger ;' ' double shake ;' 'shake of the bee ;' ' trill of the thumb ;' ' double choak,' probably the present *étouffé*, or suddenly stopping the vibration of the strings ; ' forked choaking ;' ' back of the nail ;' 'jerk ;' ' great shake.'

of what he shall obtain by the privilege of an innate Cymro; and he is a man of court, of country, and lord, and to be at the will of the court, and its judges, and its justices, during the days of the court and session, according to the regulation of law; and, for the instruction he shall impart, maintenance and gifts are due separately according to agreement.'* As we left we heard him explaining that the same ancient code declares that the advocate must take up the cause of a woman, and one born dumb.†

A real disappointment awaited us. We had specially desired to see the 'Medical Schools,' if we may so style the teaching that was given in the art of healing. The teacher and his class, however, had gone forth on a long expedition in search of some rare herbs and plants, and as our young friend had not yet entered this class he could give us little information. He told us how Samson cured an adder's bite,‡ and he gave us

---

* 'Ancient Laws and Institutions of Wales,' vol. iii., p. 512.

† 'Three persons for whom the king or the lord of the court is to assign advocates in the court; a woman or female; one that is naturally mute; and an alien ignorant of the language.' ('Ancient Laws and Institutions of Wales,' vol. ii. pp. 550-552.) We infer that little or no change in the matter of pleading was made by the great legislator of the tenth century, Howel Dda.

‡ 'Liber Landavensis.'

the names of some plants which were in repute for their medical properties. The mistletoe*—the *oll-iach* of the ancient Britons, and the *omnia sanantem* of Pliny†—was considered an antidote for all diseases. The selago, a kind of club moss,‡ was used for diseases of the eyes. The samolus or marchwort,§ for the cure of oxen and swine,‖ and many other plants associated with the art of healing.¶

We regretted not seeing the teacher of medicine and his class. We were inquisitive on many points, and we had hoped to have heard many things. We wished to know if they obtained a local and partial anæsthesia by the application of a kind of bitumen which acted through the phenol it contained. We wished to ascertain if they made decoctions of poppy and mandragora, and if they rubbed up poppy seed and henbane, and used

---

* Even Culpepper speaks of it as 'good for the grief of the sinew, itch, sores, and toothache, the biting of mad dogs and venomous beasts,' while Sir Thomas Browne alludes to its virtues in the case of epilepsy.

† 'Hist. Nat.,' lib. xxiv., s. 62.

‡ Lycopodium selago, or upright fir moss.

§ Samolus valerandi, or water pimpernel.

‖ 'Hist. Nat.,' lib. xxiv., s. 63.

¶ The author of 'Traditionary Annals of the Cymry,' says: Such are the derwen vendigaid, or vervain. . . . arian Cer, arian Gwion, bogail Gwener, boled Olwen, Bronwen, cerddinen, clych Enid, eirin Gwion, golch Enid, Ilys y dryw, meillionen olwen, pumbys yr alban, yspyddaden.'

THE OLD PLACE (LLANTWIT MAJOR).

them as a plaster to deaden the sensibility of a part to be cauterized.

The hours devoted to study were nearly over when our youthful guide asked us if we should care to visit another 'college.' We consented gladly, and he conducted us to a hall where arithmetic and mensuration were being taught. We were astonished to find that great attention was paid to the science of numbers (*rhifyddiaeth*). Number two was not considered as a plurality, because ' there cannot be a majority of numbers without three.'* We found that three was called a fixed or fundamental (*cadarn*) plurality, and its multiple — three times three, or nine — fixed pluralities, comprehending all simple numerals, which have to be repeated in conjunction with other figures, to denote ten and upwards, for 'there is no number beyond ten.'† 'Ten is the division point of numbers, and it is by tens that all numbers are arranged as far as language can give them names. Ten is the perfect circle, and ten within ten, or ten about ten, will be within and without the circumference, circle within circle for ever; therefore the best arrangement of number and numbers is ten and tens.'‡

* 'Voice Conventional of the Bards of the Isle of Britain.'
† See ' Laws of Howel Dda.'
‡ 'Coelbren y Beirdd,' by Llywelyn Sion, *apud* Iolo MSS. p. 270. 'It is remarkable,' says the author of ' The

We found several systems of numeration were in use; and the Numeration Table was drawn out to an immense length. It struck us that its length has only been equalled by the one in use among the Chinese.

The teacher of the art of measuring was extolling the virtues of Dyvnwal Moelmud, 'the best measurer,' and was saying:

'He measured this island from the promontory of Blathaon* in Prydain† to the promontory of Penwaed‡ in Cernyw, and that is nine hundred miles, the length of this island; and from Crigyll§ in Mon to Soram on the shore of Mer Udd,‖ which is five hundred miles; and that is the breadth of this island.

'The cause of his measuring this island was, that he might know the tribute of this island, the number of the miles, and its journeys in days.

Traditionary Annals of the Cymry,' 'how the doctrine of circles pervades the secular as well as the Divine sciences of the Cymry. *Cant*, a hundred, or ten times ten, literally signifies a circle.'

* Some copies of the chronicles of the kings, in which a similar passage occurs, read 'Bladon,' others 'Caithness.'

† In the text it is Prydeyn. 'Prydyn' is used to denote North Britain or Scotland.

‡ Now Penwith, in Cornwall.

§ On the west coast of Anglesey.

‖ Literally 'Lord Sea.'

'And that measure Dyvnwal measured by a barleycorn; three lengths of a barleycorn in the inch; three inches in the palm breadth; three palm breadths in the foot; three feet in the pace; three paces in the leap; three leaps in a land, the land, in modern Cymraeg, is called a ridge; and a thousand of the lands in a mile;* and that measure we still use here.†

'And they made the measure of the legal erw‡ by the barleycorn. Three lengths of a barleycorn in an inch; three inches in the palm breadth, three palm breadths in the foot; four feet in the short yoke, and eight in the field yoke, and twelve in the lateral yoke, and sixteen in the long yoke, and a rod, equal in length to that long yoke, in the hand of a driver, with the middle spike of that long yoke in the other hand of the driver, and as far as he can reach with that rod, stretching out his arm, are the two skirts of the erw, that is to say, the breadth of a legal erw; and thirty of that is the length of the erw.

* *Milltir*, i.e., *mil tir*, a thousand lands. By this computation the Cymric mile contained three miles, six furlongs, twenty-seven poles, and a yard and a half, of present measure.

† This royal measurer must have been a careful observer. He begins with the most common ingredient of human food, and then he proceeds to parts and capabilities of the human body. He must have observed very carefully to discover multiples one of another.

‡ An acre.

'Four such erws are to be in every tyddyn.*
'Four tyddyns in every randir.†
'Four randir in every trev.‡
'Four trevs in every maenol.§
'And twelve maenols and two trevs in every cymwd.‖

'The two trevs are for the use of the king; one of them to be maertrev¶ land for him; and the other to be the king's waste and summer pasture; and as much as we have said above is to be in the other cymwd, that is in number five score trevs; and that is the cantrev** rightly; ten times ten is to be in every hundred; and numeration goes no further than ten.

'This is the number of erws in the cantrev: four legal erws of tillage in every tyddyn; sixteen in every randir; sixty-four in every gavael††; two hundred and fifty-six in the trev; one thousand and twenty-four in every maenol; twelve thousand two hundred and eighty-eight in the twelve maenols. In the two trevs which pertain to the court there are to be five hundred and twelve erws; the whole of that, when summed up, is twelve thousand and eight hundred erws in the

---

* A farm or tenement. § A manor.
† A shareland. ‖ A comot.
‡ A homestead; a town. ¶ Maer vill; the demesne.
** Hundred trevs; the largest fixed division of a district.
†† A hold.

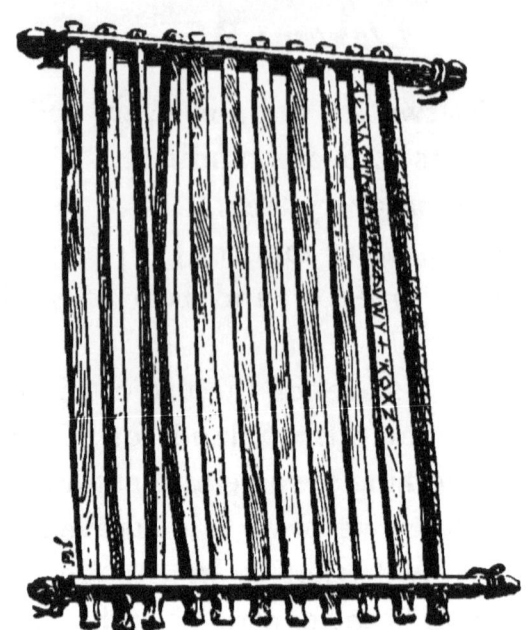

LLYFR PREN.

cymwd; and the same number in the other cymwd, that is, the number of erws in the cantrev is twenty-five thousand and six hundred, neither more nor less.'*

During this long discourse on Dyvnwal Moelmud's system of mensuration, our eyes had wandered to the other end of the hall, where we saw a class which interested us deeply. We knew that letters were originally written on wood or stone; most commonly the former; and we also knew that not only the material, but the alphabet itself, was designated 'Coelbren,' wood of credibility.† At a fitting opportunity we crossed the hall. We found the teacher of the 'Llyfr Pren,' 'Book of Tree,' had a boundless enthusiasm for his subject, and he was explaining how the hazel or mountain ash might be provided, and how each stick should be split into four quarters, and duly dried. While he was instructing his class on the mode of trimming the corners to the tenth part of an inch, we examined

* 'Ancient Laws and Institutions of Wales,' vol. i., pp. 185, 187, 189.
† 'When stone was used,' says the learned author of 'Traditionary Annals of the Cymry,' 'it was called "coelfain," the stone of credibility. Even this mode seems to have been occasionally in use down to a late period. Thus Huw Cae Llwyd (1450-1480) in his Elegy on Gwilym Tew, observes of him, that he "darllen main bychain yn ber," sweetly read the small stones.'

one of these wooden frames. We found it was an arrangement by which twelve four-sided sticks are held by two side-bars, each of which consisted of two pieces of wood tied together with thongs of leather. These sticks could be revolved, so that the 'ystorrynau,' or cuttings, as the letters were termed, could be read in succession.*

The lecturer ceased, the hours of study were over, the great doors of the hall were opened wide, and the students trooped out into the bright sunlight. We were about to follow them, when we awoke with a start, finding ourselves once more in the nineteenth century, reclining on the green sward near the gray old church of Llantwit Major.

* One specimen of the 'Llyfr Pren' is in Cardiff Museum. Mr. Storrie says 'the sticks of this "book" are made of yew, and each of their four faces is a little over a quarter of an inch in width. The side bars are of pine, and are not so well finished nor so old looking as the sticks. The letters used are known as the "Coelbren y Beirdd," or Bardic alphabet. This specimen was the property of Iolo Morganwg, who presented it to Gwilym Morganwg in 1821, the grandson of whom presented it to this museum. There is only one other known, but as it is supposed to be inscribed with Bardic secrets, I have never been able to induce its custodian to let me see it, but he states it is exactly like the Cardiff specimen, except the inscription.' (For further information see Iolo MSS., p. 617, English translation.)

CHAPTER X

CONCLUSION

CHAPTER X.

CONCLUSION.

THE glory of Bangor Illtyd soon departed. It has been remarked that its position on the coast exposed it to hostile invasions and to English influence.* In the year 959 we read of 'Saxon clerks' at Llantwit, and King Edgar, when he invaded Glamorgan, carried away the sacred bell of St. Illtyd, as well as other treasures. However, either his conscience smote him or a portent alarmed him, and he returned the plunder he had stolen. In the reign of William Rufus, Llantwit suffered severely, for Robert Fitzhamon and his band of Norman soldiers conquered a portion of South Wales, and part of the endowments of Llantwit were given by the Norman Baron to the Abbey of Tewkesbury. It was also deprived of its valued privilege of sanctuary. However, in the year 1150, Nicholas, Bishop of Llandaff, restored this right to the church of

* See Newell's 'Ancient British Church,' p. 121.

Llantwit. The appendix to the 'Legend of St. Illtyd' shows us that it had become English in sympathy, and was the object of attack from the Welshmen. We read that in Fitzhamon's time, as many as 3,000 of the Northern Welsh attacked it by night; 'if they had come by day they would have had the victory;' and it was only after a hard fight that 'the multitude of Gwynedd fled.'

The schools of learning in England acquired an ascendancy, and that of Illtyd sank into comparative obscurity.* There appears, however, to have been a school at Llantwit, which existed until it lost all its emoluments in the reign of Henry VIII.†

It was a bold experiment to establish university schools on the Glamorganshire coast a century after the death of Theodosius the Great, while the names of Alaric, Attila, and Genseric were still household words. Illtyd, however, was remarkably fitted for the work Dubricius entrusted to him. His boundless enthusiasm, tempered by the relentless discipline of a soldier's life, won from the sons of those proud nobles who flocked to his schools an admiration and respect which might not have been given to a cloistered ecclesiastic. At a time when barbarism was over-

* See Lewis' 'Topographical Dictionary of Wales.'
† 'Dr. Nichol apud Hor. Britan.,' vol. ii., p. 355.

BOVERTON (NEAR LLANTWIT MAJOR).

whelming the old civilization and a fierce struggle was taking place at many centres of Roman influence, Illtyd prepared a band of men to assist in the spiritual and intellectual organization of Wales and Armorica. Excellent indeed was the use he made of those fragments of learning he had brought with him from his native land; and although he was not an Ambrose, a Jerome, or an Augustine, yet his name and the names of many of his disciples are enshrined in the memory of a grateful people. In a sad and dreary age may we not reckon Illtyd, 'the knight,' 'the excellent master,' as one of the saviours of learning and civilization?

Elliot Stock, Paternoster Row, London.

www.ingramcontent.com/pod-product-compliance
Lightning Source LLC
Chambersburg PA
CBHW030303170426
43202CB00009B/853